PRACTIC
LIVE OR TRAVEL IN
CHINA

Ani Right

Photos by Ani Right and Public Images

Table Of Contents

Introduction   1
Planning Your Trip To China   5
The Passport And Visa   5
Procuring A Visa   6
Make A Schedule   6
Prepare According To The Weather   7
Learn The Basic Language   8
Health   8
Country's Currency   9
Traveling With Kids   9
Planning Your Itinerary   10
Packing   10
Useful Apps You Should Download When Traveling To China   12
Sim Cards In China   17
You Do Not Want To Ruin Your Trip To China!   19
Keep Yourself Safe   19
Useful Telephone Numbers   19
Did You Know?   20
Shanghai Airports   21
Beijing Capital International Airport   37
Getting Around In China   43
Public Transportation   43
Taxis   43
Sanlunche And Pedicabs   44
Cars   45
Car Rentals In China   46
Taking A Bus In China   48
Two-Wheelers Like Bikes And Scooters   52
Walk   53
High Speed Trains In China   53
Beijing–Tianjin Intercity Hsr — Best Cruise To Capital Transport   60
Local Flights In China   60
Top Hotels In China   65
1.   Amanfayun   65
2.   Jing's Residence   66
3. Grand Hyatt, Shanghai   66
4.   Kempinski Hotel, Chengdu   66
5.   Grace, Beijing   67
6.   Aman At Summer Palace, Beijing   67
7.   Park Hyatt Hotel, Beijing   67
8.   China World Hotel   68
9.   Beijing Kerry Center Hotel   68
10.   Beijing International Hotel   69
5 Best Hotels On Budget In Beijing   71
1.   Jiadejia Express Hotel   72

2.	Motel 168	72
3.	Rest Motel	72
4.	Guohan Hotel	73
5.	Aden Hotel	73

Renting An Apartment In Beijing **75**
- When Should You Start Looking For An Apartment In Beijing? — 75
- How Much Does Rent Cost In Beijing? — 76
- More About Lease Terms And Fees — 76
- How To Find An Apartment In Beijing? — 77

Western Shops, Markets In Beijing **79**
- Groceries — 79
- Fresh Products — 80
- Clothing — 81
- Household Items — 82

Chinese Restaurants **83**
- 1. Quanjude — Peking Duck — 83
- 2. South Beauty — Sichuan Cuisine — 84
- 3. Haidilao — Hotpot — 85
- 4. Morals Village — Hotpot — 86
- 5. Sichuan Folk — Sichuan Cuisine — 87
- 6. Authentic Guangzhou Food — 88
- 7. Lianxiang Lou — Moon Cake — 89
- 8. Shanghai Old Restaurant — Local Shanghai Cuisine — 89
- 9. Lvbolang — Shanghai Cuisine — 90
- 10. Louwailou — Authentic Hangzhou Dishes — 90
- 11. Zhiweiguan — Hangzhou Dessert And Snacks — 91
- 12. Jiasan Steamed Stuffed Bun Restaurant — 92

Top 5 Chinese Restaurants In Beijing **93**
- 1. Huajia Yiyuan (Hua's Restaurant) — 93
- 2. Bellagio Cafe (Gong Ti) — 94
- 3. Lost Heaven — 94
- 4. Beijing Dadong, Tian'anmen/Wangfujing — 95
- 5. Little Yunnan — 95

Top 5 Western Restaurants In Beijing **97**
- 1. The Georg — 97
- 2. Stuff'd — 98
- 3. Pebbles Courtyard — 99
- 4. Temple Restaurant — 99
- 5. Vineyard Cafe, Beijing — 100

Ordering Food In China **101**
- Reading Menus — 101

Food Delivery In Beijing **105**
- Food Delivery Services — 105
- Restaurants Having Their Own Delivery Network — 107

Organic Food In China **111**
- Home Delivery Of Organic Food In Shanghai — 111
- Suppliers — 112

Silk Street Pearl Market Beijing   **115**
Tea Street In Beijing   **119**
Dos And Dont's In China   **121**
Things To Do When In China   **127**
   1. A Version Of The Great Wall In Guiyang   127
   2. Embark On A Yangtze River Cruise   128
   3. Pay A Visit To The Terracotta Army In Xi'an   129
   4. Learn Chinese Kung Fu In Shaolin Temple   130
   5. See The Giant Pandas In The Sichuan Province   130
   6. Learn To Cook Chinese Food   131
   7. Visit "798 Art District" In Beijing   132
   8. Celebrate The Chinese New Year (Spring Festival)   132
   9: Do Some Shopping In Hong Kong   132
Things Considered Unlucky In China   **135**
What To Buy In China   **137**
   Top Souvenirs For A First-Time Traveler To China   138
   Glasses And Contacts   138
   Accessories And Jewelry   139
   Tailoring And Clothes   139
   Leather Goods   139
Toilets In China   **141**
   China Travel Tips On Toilets   141
Credit Cards And Cash In China   **143**
Must See In Beijing   **145**
   The Great Wall Of China   145
   The Forbidden City   146
   Must See Shows In Beijing   147
Travel Agencies In China   **153**
Chinese Massage   **155**
   Chinese Massage Techniques   156
Invitations To Drink Tea   **161**
   Tea Serving Etiquette In China   162
Socializing In China   **165**
   1. 麻将 (Má Jiang) – Mahjong   165
   2. Do It Like A 东北人 (Dōng Běi Rén) – Northeasterner: Streetside Barbecue And Beer   166
   3. Ultimate Social Food: 火锅 (Huǒ Guō) – Hotpot   167
   4. Ktv: It's Not Karaoke Like We Know It   168
Tv Channels In China 169
   1. Cctv 中央电视台   169
   2. Hunan Satellite Television 湖南卫视   169
   3. Phoenix Satellite Television 凤凰卫视   170
   4. Shanghai Oriental Television 东方卫视   170

5. Jiangsu Satellite Television 江苏卫视 170

6. Zhejiang Television 浙江卫视 170

7. Shenzhen Satellite Tv 深圳卫视 171

8. The Travel Channel 旅游卫视 171

9. Anhui Tv 安徽卫视 171

10. Xing Kong Tv 星空卫视 171

Finding An Ayi - Or A Babysitter In China **173**
Things To Consider 173
Ways Of Finding An Ayi Or Babysitter 173
Interviewing Your Potential Ayi Or Babysitter 174
Your Obligations 175
Smoking In China **177**
Scam Alerts To Look Out For In China **179**
The Art School Scam 179
The Fake Taxi Ride 180
Tea House Scam 180
Shopping Scams 181
Leaving China **183**
Documents To Prepare When Leaving China 183
Conclusion **187**
Interested In Getting My Books For Free? **188**
How To Apply? 188

INTRODUCTION

I moved to China three years ago. When preparing to relocate, I was looking for practical tips or advice, books that could help me understand what to expect. Frankly speaking, I did not find many. However, my research on the Internet was more successful. I came across some good articles but could not find a comprehensive, concise, and practical handbook on China. So now, after my personal experiences living and traveling in China, I have decided to write this book. My hope is that it might be helpful to anyone planning to relocate or just looking to spend a few days or weeks in China. Here you will find everything you need to know for your trip, starting with what you need to prepare, what to avoid, dos and don'ts, popular scams, how to get around, as well as main places to eat, to live, and so on.

Lhasa Potala Palace

I am really surprised to see so few foreigners when I travel in throughout provinces in China, mostly I am surrounded by local tourists. Maybe this lack of international tourism is because information in other languages is missing. Or perhaps the available information doesn't look quite right as it was translated by Google/Baidu (Chinese Google) translate. I would encourage anyone to visit this beautiful country and its provinces, which are so diverse and yet sometimes look so little similar to one another. I can frankly confess that my favorite province is Yunnan, with its rich and stunning nature, diverse minority culture, and its delicious cuisine. China boasts not only the Great Wall and Emperor Qin Shi Huang's Terracotta Army, but so much more.

Leaping Tiger Gorge

I like this country a lot, and I hope this book will help you to feel confident as you organize your next trip to China!

Chaoyang Park in Beijing

PLANNING YOUR TRIP TO CHINA

China is a beautiful country with an extensive history. Besides its mind blowing architectural sites and landscapes, it has a rich culture and great gastronomy. These factors contribute to why China is one of the most visited places in the world.

However, when visiting a new destination, it is essential to have a clear picture of what you want and expect from a trip, as this will help in the preparation. Contained in this book are a lot of useful facts that will help you make informed decisions about traveling to China.

There are so many things that are involved when planning a trip to China. Each country has its own travel policies, and this also applies to China. American and European citizens do not need to acquire a visa before traveling to most countries, but you need to get a visa if you want to travel to China. Getting a visa is one of the most important items on the checklist of things to do.

THE PASSPORT AND VISA

Now that you are aware that you need to have a valid passport to visit China, you also need to know where to apply for an appropriate visa. Visas are processed and issued at any Chinese embassy or consulate serving your country.

PROCURING A VISA

To procure a visa, you can either schedule an appointment at the Chinese embassy or consulate to have them help you go through the necessary steps to get a visa, or you can ask your travel agent to manage the process for you. And if you wish to avoid the sometimes-cumbersome process, you can employ the services of a special visa agent, which you can find on Google, at an extra cost.

MAKE A SCHEDULE

Regardless of the length of your stay in China, it is very important to make a schedule. Even if you are not entirely sure about the places you want to visit, you need to have a rough idea of the cities you want to travel to. This is incredibly important because China is a huge country. From highly populated cities to deserts and from mountain ranges to extensive forests, China has a lot to offer. In order to avoid confusion regarding the variety of tourist spots available, you must be sure about your preferences.

Guiyang old city

Planning your schedule, therefore, is key. Obviously, you don't want to waste your holiday wondering where to go in China!

PREPARE ACCORDING TO THE WEATHER

One of the reasons China is such a great vacation spot is its weather. Several cities in China experience mild weather throughout the year, making them perfect for a vacation in every season. Ideally, China should be visited during spring or autumn. It is imperative to check the weather conditions of the cities you are visiting and to prepare accordingly. This is because the country is huge and different cities have different temperatures. Winter temperatures can drop to -40°C in areas like Inner

Mongolia. On the other hand, areas like Hong Kong can be as hot as 38°C in the summers. Therefore, if you are planning to travel around to more than one city, make sure you check the local weather for each city and prepare accordingly.

LEARN THE BASIC LANGUAGE

Yes, almost everyone is learning to speak English these days; however, China is one of the countries where you will come across people who speak nothing but their mothertongue – which in this case is likely Mandarin Chinese. You would not want a language barrier to ruin your trip. Therefore, it is a great idea to learn a few basic words that will help you ask for directions. You can also download the **ITranslate** app before leaving.

HEALTH

When taking a trip to a new locale, it doesn't hurt to take precautions and find out the latest news and happenings when it comes to health issues. The majority of countries do not require any kind of vaccinations before going to China, but they do make some recommendations, so be sure to look at the consular website section of your Ministry of Foreign Affairs. It is also important to look at the major ingredients of popular foods, in case of allergies.

COUNTRY'S CURRENCY

The official currency in China is the Renminbi (RMB), which is also known as the Chinese Yuan (CNY). Having a little knowledge about the denomination of the Chinese currency will be useful on your trip. Learn in advance how to distinguish main bank notes or coins so you feel confident, and also make sure to exchange some money before the trip; it will help make payment easier, especially on the first day of your trip.

TRAVELING WITH KIDS

Traveling with kids? No problem. Though it can be stressful, it can be more fun than frustrating with adequate planning and preparation. Being prepared is a must when you've got kids to travel with, so make things easy on yourself. Knowing what kinds of activities are available for the little ones when they get bored of seeing temples and monuments is also helpful.

Make sure to bring all the essentials that will make your kids feel comfortable and settled in the new environment. Incorporate awesome kid's activities into the trip, but check for availability and make arrangements in advance.

PLANNING YOUR ITINERARY

A Colorful Miao Minority

So as to have a proper itinerary, put in writing all of those places you have dreamed of seeing in China. The options are inexhaustible, and there is a place for every personality. You could take a hiking tour of the Great Wall, experience a Chinese high-speed rail ride, take a Panda tour or explore the minority's culture in Yunnan province, there are just so many things to do, you won't be bored.

PACKING

Personally, I don't feel there is a need to do any heavy packing. Just bring stuff that is essential and you won't easily be able to get in the new environment. The trip is an opportunity to buy new and unique things.

Do not pack valuables (passport, laptop, money, camera, etc.) in your checked bag. Pack the minimum amount of items you think you'll need—then reduce by half. Remember, you're responsible for your personal belongings throughout the trip. Clothes can be layered and laundry can be done, if necessary. Pack any item that might be considered a weapon (razors, scissors, Swiss Army knives, etc.) in your checked bag. Matches or lighters of any type are prohibited on all Chinese flights in checked luggage as well. Liquids and gels must also be packed in your checked bag. Carry-on liquids or gels must be in 3 oz. containers or smaller and all must fit in one single quart-size clear plastic bag. Place this bag in a bin at the security checkpoint for screening.

Some packing hints:

1. Pack your passport, medications, valuables, travel documents, and everything you'll need for one night (change of clothes, small toiletries) in your carry-on bag.
2. Pack tightly, rolling or folding your clothes. Leave ample space for souvenirs and gifts. Bring an outfit suitable for a nice evening out.
3. Pack according to the season and climate. Check local weather conditions online. In warm weather, shorts are fine for most sightseeing venues but not in religious sites. Bring a sweater or jacket or a warm scarf for cool evenings and air conditioned premises, and

protection from rain and sun (compact umbrella, sunblock, sunglasses, hat, etc.)

4. Pack (or wear) a good pair of comfortable, broken-in walking shoes. Bring a second, nicer pair for a dinner or show.

5. Bring a backpack to carry during day trips. Always carry tissues, moist towelettes or hand sanitizer and toilet paper.

6. Consider packing a single use or digital camera, battery and cell phone chargers, alarm clock, extra plastic bags, and high fiber snacks.

USEFUL APPS YOU SHOULD DOWNLOAD WHEN TRAVELING TO CHINA

Are you familiar with apps? Well, there are several handy mobile tools that can make a difference during your trip to China. These applications are useful to travelers, and they come with various functions like language translation, directions, traveling, finding taxis, or restaurants and so much more. Below are some apps that perform these functions.

LANGUAGE APPS

Pleco Chinese Dictionary

Pleco is a Chinese learning companion. The app is described as "an integrated dictionary/ document reader/ flashcard system with fullscreen handwriting input and live OCR, from a company that's been making the world's best mobile Chinese learning apps since 2001." It's the go-to app if you can't read things such as menus, signs, or can't translate a tourist attraction name into Chinese.

HelloChinese - Learn Chinese Mandarin

This application is the best for a beginner learning Mandarin Chinese. It is a game-based Chinese learning app that features: systematic courses based on levels, a well-designed Pinyin (pronunciation) course for newbies, innovative self-adaptive learning games that incorporate Chinese cultural education, and a bite-sized curriculum to fortify your Chinese listening, speaking, reading, and writing skills. For more functional features, you have to pay $4.99 for the upgraded version, which also includes vocabulary lists, accommodation listings, shopping information, regions and towns, countries, tourist attractions, family, dating sites, hospitals, and more.

NAVIGATION APPS

Google Maps

Google Maps is the most comprehensive map service throughout the world. As it is fully available in English and any language of choice, it makes it easy to navigate around even if you don't speak the local language. Presently, this Google-powered service still works with a VPN-enabled device.

China Travel Guide (Free)

The China Travel guide offers you a complete city guide for over 100 cities in China, including Beijing, Shanghai, and Xian. It is a travel guide that includes: a sightseeing section with all major monuments, an offline map, a phrasebook, and listings for restaurants, bars, pubs, and nightlife. This app is not only easy to use, but it also works offline.

TRANSPORT APPS

China Metro (Free)

This is your one stop app when it comes to subway information in China. This is the only application that supports all 15 cities having metro systems in Greater China Region. It has full offline support through online update supported. It contains route maps for metro and light rail, station info, first-last train departure, the fare for all routes, GPS location, and more.

Taxi! China ($1.99)

Taxi! China is perfect for a traveler headed to China. With over 10,000 locations across major and smaller cities in China, you can get just about anywhere. This app contains information about everywhere you might want to go: hotels, airports, malls, convention centers, tourist attractions, and many other places. It has lists of important phrases and phone numbers so that you'll never be lost.

SOCIAL APPS

WeChat (Free)

WeChat is a messaging and calling application that allows you to easily connect with family and friends across countries. WeChat is the most popular messaging service in China, and is just right for staying connected to not just old friends but to new friends made on the trip. You can send texts and voice messages, and you can call people for free if you're both connected to either Wi-Fi, 3G or 4G. In China, everyone uses it – for chatting, paying your bills, navigating around. I would recommend downloading it as you will constantly be asked what your WeChat account is. I use it for many purposes even in museums. It is very handy to communicate with your guide as well.

TRAVEL HELP APPS

Flight Radar

Not only does this app turn your device into a personal air traffic radar or flight tracker, but it also provides full details on every aspect of air travel. Getting around by air doesn't get any easier than with this application.

Dianping

The main restaurant review site in China also created an application, known as "dianping." It is indeed useful in finding great restaurants, plus it also contains ratings for these restaurants from other customers. Though not all of these reviews are available in English, the basic information is provided in English, and the Chinese address makes it convenient to ask people how to get there (for example, just hand over the dianping review for wherever you want to go, either to a driver or a local, and you'll quickly be on your way).

AIR QUALITY APPS

PureSky or **Beijing Air Quality** apps are helpful apps for checking the air quality in China. You must have heard about air pollution in China; these apps will help you to know when you are supposed to use masks to protect yourself from the pollution. Consider buying a mask with a filter in advance or upon arrival at SOS International. It costs around 200 RMB, but I strongly recommend not only to buy it, but to use it when recommended. Check the app for recommendations every day.

VPNs

In China, some applications are not automatically functional; for example, Facebook, Instagram, Snapchat, and Twitter are not useable unless you have a VPN downloaded onto your phone. A VPN helps to auto configure your settings and sometimes go around a firewall, to help you access certain apps. There are various downloadable VPNs to choose from. If you want to use Gmail, Hotmail, etc., and live your life as usual while in China, then downloading a VPN is a must. I bought mine one week after I moved to China, and it was a huge relief.

SIM CARDS IN CHINA

There are 3 main network providers in China: China Mobile, China Unicom, and China Telecom. Before heading to China, please make sure that your mobile is unlocked and that you can use a Chinese SIM card. From the experience of my friends and my own, I would recommend China Unicom SIM card Basic 3G Voice/ Data SIM. It costs 66 RMB and is monthly prepaid. For this price, you get 50 minutes of outgoing calls, 240 outgoing SMS, 300 MGB of 3G data. You can get this card in any China Unicom store or a mobile phone vendor. China Unicom and China Mobile have shops in Terminal 3 of Beijing Capital Airport, near the luggage carousels.

YOU DO NOT WANT TO RUIN YOUR TRIP TO CHINA!

There is just so much to do in China that it can actually become quite overwhelming. As it is going to be a new experience, try to take it in, one breath at a time. In most things, employ the rule of moderation. As with any new country and culture, there might be some annoyances or irritations. Don't let this get you down!

KEEP YOURSELF SAFE

It is imperative to be proactive and vigilant. In many situations, safety is a given and you can expect hospitable treatment from the locals. However, as in any other country, do beware of pickpockets in crowded places. Never show off your flashy accessories and be sure to secure your bags and pouches where you can prominently see them. As a foreigner, you also have to take precautions not to fall for scams and do not stay out too late as you are not familiar with the environment yet.

USEFUL TELEPHONE NUMBERS

Fire 119

First Aid 120

Police Station 110

Report a Traffic Accident 122

DID YOU KNOW?

That keeping your hotel room card with you wherever you go is helpful in getting directions back to your hotel should you get lost?

When taking a taxi, it is a must to have your destination and its address written down in Chinese characters so you can show it to your driver?

That there is a lot more to think about when traveling to China, and this is just the tip of the iceberg? It is an amazingly beautiful country that you have to see! Whether it's the countryside or the busy city, your travels in China will open your mind to new adventures and insights.

SHANGHAI AIRPORTS

1. SHANGHAI PUDONG INTERNATIONAL AIRPORT

LOCATION

Shanghai Pudong International Airport is located in Pudong New District, about 18.6 miles (30 kilometers) from the downtown area and about 24.9 miles (40 kilometers) from Hongqiao International Airport.

BRIEF INTRO

Covering an area of more than 15.4 square miles (40 square kilometers), Pudong Airport is one of China's most famous and important airports. The more than 197.7 acres meters (800,000 square) of parking aprons along with 76 gate positions provide evidence of its importance.

This airport also consists of two terminal buildings, free shuttle buses, and special roadways that connect the two terminals. There are also thirteen baggage transfer belts for arrivals and twenty-eight boarding bridges. Other services, such as shopping areas and restaurants, are also available to provide travelers with more convenience and comfort during their stay. Currently, airlines flying in and out of Pudong airport provide services to 62 domestic cities and 73 international destinations.

TRANSPORT BETWEEN PUDONG AIRPORT AND CITY CENTER

•   SHUTTLE BUS: Ten airport bus lines handle transfers from Pudong International Airport to the city center.

•   MAGLEV: Maglev Train operates between Pudong International Airport and Longyang Rd. There is a train depart from PVG Subway Station every day from 06:45 to 21:40 at intervals of 15 to 20 minutes. The whole journey takes only eight minutes. The charge is CNY 50 for an ordinary single trip, CNY 100 for VIP, CNY 80 for an ordinary round trip, and CNY 160 for VIP. You can buy an ordinary single ticket at a preferential price of CNY 40 if you have an intraday air ticket. When you get off at Longyang Rd. Station, you can transfer to Subway Line 2 running westward and pass by many of the city's prosperous areas such as Century Park, Lujiazui, East Nanjing Road, and People's Square.

•   SUBWAY LINE 2: Subway Line 2 is a long and busy line connecting Pudong and Puxi. After extentions, it now stretches to PVG, led to Hongiao Airport either. Passengers have to get off the 4-car metro train at Guanglan Road Station (between Longyang Road Station and PVG) and then change another 8-car metro train to go ahead. Vice versa, passengers get off at the same subway station from an 8-car train and get on a 4-car train to enter Pudong Airport. It costs CNY9 for the whole trip and CNY8 from Pudong to Hongqiao airport. It takes more than one hour to travel between the two airports.

144-HOUR VISA-FREE TRANSIT

Citizens of 53 countries and regions can travel to Pudong and Hongqiao Airports without a transit visa if the period of stay does not exceed 144 hours, you can show a valid passport, have a visa for your destination country, and hold a connecting flight ticket. If you fulfill these criteria, you are allowed to leave the airport.

The countries included in this arrangement are: Albania, Argentina, Austria, Australia, Belarus, Belgium, Bosnia and Herzegovina, Brazil, Brunei, Bulgaria, Canada, Chile, Croatia, Cyprus, Czech Republic, Denmark, Estonia, Finland, France, Germany, Greece, Hungary, Iceland, Ireland, Italy, Japan, Latvia, Lithuania, Luxembourg, Macedonia, Malta, Mexico, Monaco, Netherlands, New Zealand, Poland, Portugal, Qatar, Republic of Montenegro, Romania, Russia, Serbia, Singapore, Slovakia, Slovenia, South Korea, Spain, Sweden, Switzerland, United Arab Emirates, Ukraine, United Kingdom, and United States.

Passengers can not only transit in this city, but they can also transit in Hangzhou Xiaoshan Airport and Nanjing Lukou Airport. During the six days, they can travel throughout the Shanghai, Zhejiang, and Jiangsu Provinces.

Visas are not necessary for cabin staff and passengers from any other countries who come to China and will only stay within the airport for no more than 24 hours.

PASSENGER TRANSFER

T2 has three floors. Domestic departure and arrival are mixed on Level 1. Passengers will need no more than 20 minutes to finish the whole procedure of transfer between one domestic flight to another.

There is a transfer hall of 4,000 square meters in the center of the building, equipped with forty counters to handle centralized services for ticketing, border and security inspection, and baggage checking. It is extremly convenient for those passengers who will be transferring between domestic (D) and international (I) flights and I - I flights.

- I - D: After arriving in the CIQ (China Inspection & Quarantine) Area and being checked, head for the transfer hall to handle check-in and enter the concourse of departure (minimum time duration is approximately 51 minutes).

- D - I: After arriving to the connected concourse and passing through the domestic departure area, head for the transfer hall and take an escalator or elevator up to the international CIQ Area, preparing for departure (minimum time duration about 49 minutes).

- I - I: There are nine counters to handle the transfer and transit service in the central part of the international arrival concourse. After arranging the boarding check, take the dedicated elevator up to the international CIQ Area to await departure (minimum time duration about 29 minutes).

AIRPORT FACILITIES & SERVICES

1. **SHOPPING AREA**: For your convenience, duty-free shopping is also available between Gates 15 and 20 for International Departures.

2. **RESTAURANTS**: Dozens of restaurants can be found within the airport. Two of the most famous establishments are Canglang Ting Restaurant and Hong Fangzi Western Food Restaurant.

3. **HOURLY HOTEL**: A three-star-rated hotel is located on the Transfer Level of the main terminal building. You will need to provide your boarding pass before registering.

4. **SMOKING AREAS**: You are not allowed to smoke in the airport. The smoking areas are set up outside the terminal buildings: two at T1 and three at T3. The entrances of the smoking areas are as follows:

AIRPORT CLINIC

T1: Boarding Gate no. 200-203, Domestic Departure Hall; Boarding Gate no. 213-216, International Departure Hall.

T2: Boarding Gate no. 219-221 & no. 222-224, Domestic Departure Hall; the Terrace of the Corridor at International Departure Hall.

1. **TOILETS**: Restrooms are conveniently located in both the Domestic Departure area as well as the International Departure areas.

2. **CLINIC**: In the event of a need for medical attention, the airport has medical clinics in the following locations:

3) Room A2-210, 2 F, Domestic Arrivals

Tel: 021-68345328

2) Between Gate 6 and Gate 7, Domestic Departures

Tel: 021-68345376

3) Room C2-213, 2 F, International Arrivals

TICKETING: For your convenience, Shanghai Airlines, China Eastern Airlines, and China Southern Airlines have offices located within Pudong International Airport.

INFORMATION: There are two information counters located within Pudong International Airport. One is between Gate 3 and Gate 4 in Domestic Departures area, and the other is between Gate 11 and Gate 12 in International Departures area.

LOST & FOUND: A lost and found office is located near No.7 Gate in the Arrivals area. The lost and found telephone number is 021-68346324

BANK: For your banking convenience, banks are located in the following areas:

Pudong Development Bank: between Gate 10 and Gate 12 in International Arrivals area.

Bank of China: between Gate 15 and Gate 16 in International Departures area.

Industrial & Commercial Bank of China: between Gate 12 and Gate 14 in International Departures area.

China Citic Bank: between Gate 4 and Gate 5 in Domestic Departures area.

BAGGAGE CLAIM AND INQUIRES

Address: south of International Arrivals Baggage Claim Area

AIRPORT POLICE: The Pudong International Airport Police telephone numbers are 021-6834565 and 021-68345692.

2. *SHANGHAI HONGQIAO INTERNATIONAL AIRPORT*

LOCATION

Shanghai Hongqiao International Airport is situated in the western outskirts of the city, about 8 miles (13 kilometers) from the downtown area and about 37 miles (60 kilometers) from Pudong International Airport.

BRIEF INTRO

Being the first civilian airport in this city, Hongqiao Airport is more than eighty years old. After a series of renovations, it has become one of the top three international air transit centers in China. Ninety-one airlines currently fly out of here to both domestic and international cities.

Terminal 1 is comprised of Zone A and Zone B, which covers about 20.3 acres (82,000 square meters) with 15 waiting halls, 18 VIP lounges, and 15 baggage transfer belts. After extension, in addition to a new terminal, there is a new runway of 3300 meters and a new set of associated facilities. The newly built runway is applicable for the largest aircrafts, including A380.

AIRLINES

Since March 16, 2010, fourteen airlines use the new terminal (T2). They are Hainan Airlines, Hebei Airlines, Juneyao Airlines, China United Airlines, Shandong Airlines, Shanghai Airlines, Shenzhen Airlines, Sichuan Airlines, Tianjin Airlines, Tibet Airlines, Xiamen Airlines, China Eastern Airlines, Air China, and China Southern Airlines.

In T1, there are thirteen airlines: Korean Air, Air Macau, Dragon Air, Asiana Airlines, Japan Airlines, Eva Air, TransAsia Airways, All Nippon Airways, Hong Kong Airlines, Spring Airlines, China Eastern Airlines, Air China, China Airlines.

PASSENGER TRANSFER

For passengers with boarding passes for connecting flights:

Walk to Transfer Hall - enter transfer area - Departure Hall - Boarding Gate

For passengers without a through boarding pass:

Walk to Transfer Hall - enter transfer area - check-in again at transfer counter - Departure Hall - Boarding Gate.

For passengers who have to handle lugguage by themselves:

Get to 1F to claim lugguage - transfer counter on 1F – check in again – up to 2F by escalator – Departure Hall by elevator – Boarding Gate.

TRANSPORT BETWEEN TERMINALS

It has its runways in the middle and terminal buildings on two sides. It is a waste of time to walk from one to another if you go to the wrong terminal. There are free shuttle buses running between terminals. They run every few minutes, and it takes 15 minutes between T1 and T2.

Pick-up points:

South side of Gate 6, Departure Hall, T1

North side of Gate 1, Arrival Hall, T2

Hours: 06:30-23:00

Frequency: every 15 minutes, 5 minutes in peak hours

TRANSPORT BETWEEN HONGQIAO AIRPORT AND CITY CENTER

i. SHUTTLE BUS

Bus routes at T1: 807, 806 and 1207

Bus routes at T2: Shuniu Line 4, Shuniu Line 9, Airport Bus Line 1 and 941 during the daytime; night lines are 316.

ii. TAXI

The taxi fare from Hongqiao International Airport to People's Square in the city center is approximately CNY60 and it takes about half an hour. A taxi from Hongqiao International Airport to Xujiahui, a bustling commercial area in Xuhui District, costs about CNY 40-50 and takes 20 minutes.

Pick-up point:

Exit of the Arrival Hall, T1

South side of Gate 4, Arrival Hall, T2

Special Notes: Not easy to get a taxi in peak hours.

iii. SUBWAY

Subway Line 2 and Line 10 connect the two terminals of Hongqiao Airport to the city center and further to Pudong Airport. Passengers can use these two subway lines to Hongqiao Railway Station, Yuyuan Garden, Jing'an Temple, People's Square, Nanjing East Road, Lujiazui, Longyang Road, and Pudong International Airport directly from Hongqiao Airport. Subway station is in the basement of the terminal building.

Tips: Passengers who take Subway Line 2 have to get off at Guanglan Road Subway Station and transfer from an 8-car train to a 4-car train to continue on to Pudong Airport.

The city has adopted the 144-Hour Visa-Free Transit policy. The policy is available to the citizens of 53 countries and regions under the condition that they fly in and fly out within 144 hours. Passengers are allowed to travel in Shanghai, Hangzhou, or Nanjing rather than be limited to stay in the transit city.

FACILITIES

SHOPPING AND DINING

T1: Stores are in Departures Hall, including A3, A4, A6, and A8, and Waiting Hall. Food halls are mainly distributed in A4 and A5, as well as the Waiting Hall.

T2: Departure level (M2) and ticketing & check-in level (3F)

CLINICS

T1: Near the Security Check-in Domestic Departures Hall on 2F

On the right of Domestic Arrivals on 1F

T2: Between Boarding Gate 47 and 48, M2 (Hours: 07:30-last flight)

Beside the Transfer Area, 2F (Hours: 08:30-17:30)

Besides the Lugguage Locker, Arrivals Hall, 1F (Hours: 06:30-22:00)

BUSINESS CENTER

You are provided with a computer, fax, copy, internet, telephone, and other services.

T1: A5 Waiting Hall, Departures Hall

Beside the Baggage Storage Area in Departures Hall

Beside B11 First-Class Cabin Lounge in Departures Hall

Business hours: 07:30-19:00, 07:00-18:30

T2: Business triangle area in M2

Business hours: following the flight times

SMOKING AREAS

T2 of Shanghai Hongqiao Airport

T2 of Hongqiao Airport Outdoor smoking areas are available.

T1: 2 sites. The entrances are at Boarding Gate B1, Domestic Departure Hall, and Boarding Gate B17, International Departure Hall.

T2: 2 sites. The entrances are at Boarding Gate no. 41 & 54, Domestic Departure Hall.

LOUNGES

Lounges for the old, the weak, the pregnant, and the disabled.

T1: A5, B12 Waiting Hall, departures level

Opening hours: 07:00 - 18:00

First-class cabin lounge: 2F Waiting Halls, Opening hours: 08:30 - 18:00

T2: widely distributed on 1F, 2F, M2 and two on 3F

VIP Lounge: one opposite the Security Check on 3F

Room V1-3 next to Boarding Gate 24, M2

Room 4-6 next to the Information Desk

PRAM FOR BABIES: There is a service counter on M2 level. Pram is offered free of charge.

SERVICES

TICKETING

T1:

Honqiao Airport: 211-214 counters, Departures Hall

Tel: 021-51146655

Arrivals Hall, Building B

Tel: 021-51142078

Shanghai Airlines: Counters 202-206, Check-in Hall, Departures Hall

China Eastern Airlines: Counters 251-255, Check-in Hall, Departures Hall

China Southern Airlines: Counters 206, 261 and 266, Departures Hall

T2: Check-in & Ticketing Hall, 3F (China Eastern, Air China, China Southern, Shenzhen, Hainan, Xiamen, Shandong, Spring and Juneyao Airlines as well as Hongqiao Airport all have ticketing counters here).

CHECK-IN COUNTERS

T1:

Air China: Counters 262 and 263, Departures Hall

China Southern Airlines: Counters 105-107, Departures Hall

T2:

Counters A01-A13 (Xiamen, Shandong, Hainan, Juneyao and Sichuan and Tianjin Airlines)

Counters A14-A21(China Air)

Counters B01-B18 (Shenzhen Airlines)

Counters C01-C18, D01-D10 (China Eastern Airlines)

Counters D11-D15 (China Southern Airlines)

Shanghai Airlines and China Eastern Airlines share the same check-in counters. They have totally 48 check-in counters and 28 check-in machines in Terminal 2. Passengers of the two airlines can handle check-in at any of those 48 counters.

BATTERY CAR:

Service counter can be found on M2. Battery cars make it easy to get around T2.

LEFT & LOST LUGGAGE T1:

Lost & Found: Beside Gate 1, Arrivals Hall

Tel: 021-51142071

Baggage Storage: beside Gate 5, Arrivals Hall

Tel: 021-51144520

Gate 5, Departures Hall

Tel: 021-51144553

T2: Lost luggage, Lost & Found services are at the same counters available in Arrivals Hall and E Island, East Traffic Center, 1F

Tel: 021-22381086 (Lost & Found); 021-22381085 (left-lugguage)

Hours: 8:00-21:3

BEIJING CAPITAL INTERNATIONAL AIRPORT

BRIEF INTRO

Beijing Capital International Airport

Beijing Capital International Airport is situated in the Shunyi District of the city of Beijing, about 25 km (about 15.5 miles) northeast of Tiananmen Square, and it is China's busiest and most important international airport. It consists of three terminal buildings. The airport's high standard of services and facilities has attracted 66 airlines to operate here. Currently, the airport has flight connections to 88 domestic and 69 foreign airports.

72 HOURS VISA - FREE TRANSIT

This transit is appropriate for transit passengers in Beijing and 17 other cities in China. Passengers from 51 countries can enjoy the 72 hour visa if they are from one of the 24 Schengen agreement countries: Ireland, Cyprus, Bulgaria, Romania, the United Kingdom, Russia, Croatia, Serbia, Macedonia (FYROM), Montenegro, Bosnia-Herzegovina, Albania, the U.S., Canada, Brazil, Mexico, Argentina, Chile, Australia, New Zealand, Republic of Korea, Japan, Singapore, Brunei Darussalam, United Arab Emirates, and Qatar.

Please note that passengers transiting in Beijing are not allowed to leave the administrative area of the city.

CAPITAL AIRPORT TRANSFER

Airport pick-up and see-off services with professional drivers are available from Beijing Capital Airport.

1. From Jan. 1, 2013, passport holders of 51 countries and regions are granted a visa-free stay of up to 72 hours when taking an international transfer via Capital Airport.

2. Since April 15, 2015, transit passengers from any country/region can stay in the airport's transit area for up to 24 hours without going through border inspections. However, both the arrival and connecting flights need to be international, either from/to a third country/region or their home country/region.

For the sake of the privacy of females, PEK considerately sets privileged passes for female passengers' security check at T1, T2, and T3. You can find obvious marks with "Female Only" at the Security Check Channel.

TERMINAL 1 OF CAPITAL AIRPORT

Occupying an area of 60,000 square meters, Terminal 1 has the longest history originating from January 1980. While the larger T2 and T3 terminals were put into use successively, T1 has always been the operational base for Hainan Airlines' domestic flights. Currently, there is a convenient passage linking T1 and T2, which just takes 5 minutes on foot.

Beijing Capital Airport Airline Companies in T1

Beijing-Shanghai Air Express, Capital Airlines (JD), Grand China Airlines Domestic (CN), Hainan Airlines Domestic (HU), Tianjin Airlines (GS)

TERMINAL 2 OF CAPITAL AIRPORT

Covering an area of 336,000 square meters, T2 was originally built in October 1995, and put into use in November 1999. Although it is the extension project for T1, T2 was built much larger than the previous one. Before the opening of T3, it played a vital role in aerial transportation throughout China. Currently, T2 is the busiest terminal of the airport, taking on the domestic airlines to and from this city; although, Air China in T3 supplies frequent domestic flights. On the other hand, housing over 30 international airlines companies, this terminal is also one of the major ports for passengers seeking entry into and exit from China.

TERMINAL 3 OF CAPITAL AIRPORT

T3 of Airport has been attracting a great deal of public attention since coming into use in 2008. It has a unique modern design and is the second largest airport terminal in the world, only after Terminal 3 of the Dubai International Airport. Some 26 national and international airlines have moved into this building, which runs 2900 meters long from north to south.

AIRPORT TRANSPORTATION

i.   Airport Express Train

The Airport Express Line of the Subway serves the airport from Terminal 3 to Terminal 2, and then takes passengers to Dongzhimen via Sanyuanqiao. This train line was opened just prior to the 2008 Summer Olympics. It carries passengers to the airport in twenty minutes from the city center, covering a distance of 28 kilometers.

ii.   Airport Shuttle Bus

Currently, there are nine different shuttle bus routes connecting the airport with various locations in the downtown area, including Xidan, Railway Station, West Railway Station, Nanyuan Airport and others.

Airport Intercity Bus

•   Capital Airport—Tianjin City

- Capital Airport—Tanggu, Tianjin City

- Captial Airport—Langfang City

- Capital Airport—Baoding City

- Capital Airport—Qinhuangdao City

- Capital Airport—Tangshan City

To simplify transportation to and from nearby Tianjin City and Qinhuangdao City, five intercity bus lines have been opened between the Capital Airport and these two cities.

CROSS TERMINAL FREE SHUTTLE BUS

Every seven minutes, there is a free shuttle bus leaving from Terminal 3 for Terminal 2 and then Terminal 1, and vice versa. The bus takes just 15 minutes one-way.

Pick-up stations: T1 – Gate3-5 on the 1st Floor; T2 – Gate 11 on the 1st Floor; T3 – Gate 5 on the 1st Floor

Route: Gate 5 of T3 Arrival Floor→T2 Departure Floor→T1 Departure Floor→Gate 11 of T2 Arrival Floor→Gate 5 of T1 Arrival Floor→T3 Departure Floor→Gate 5 of T3 Arrival Floor

Operating hours: every 10 minutes at 06:00~23:00; every 30 minutes at 23:00~06:00 (the next day)

   iii. TAXI

Official Taxi Stands: T1, outside Gate no. 1, 1F; T2, outside Gate no. 5-9, 1F; T3, outside of the terminal building (please follow the clear signage to find it).

Consulting Hotline: 010-64558892

Source: www.travelchinaguide.com

Tips:

1. Any possible fee for the journey should be paid by the passenger.

2. Do take the official taxis at the sites mentioned above. It should be noted that queuing up is sometimes needed.

3. It is suggested to ask for the taxi receipt before getting out in case of any trouble. It is very important to ask the driver to use the meter for the ride.

GETTING AROUND IN CHINA

There are many different ways to get around in China, most are easy to use and inexpensive.

PUBLIC TRANSPORTATION

Car ownership is still in its infancy in China – I know, it's hard to believe this when you witness the traffic in Beijing and many other places throughout China. But because so few people own a car, public transportation is very well developed with an extensive network of subways and buses.

Beijing Public Transportation IC Card. There is no monthly pass or multi-day ticket but you can buy a rechargeable IC card, the so-called Yikatong 一卡通, which can be used for both subway and buses. If you use public transportation regularly, the Yikatong is certainly the way to go. You can buy it at many of the bigger subway stations. Look for the blue sign that says IC Card.

TAXIS

Again, because so few people have cars, taxis are a very common and cheap form of transportation in Beijing. Read more on *taking a fake taxi.*

SANLUNCHE AND PEDICABS

Beijing Transportation SanluncheSanlunche, literally "Three-wheel-car," are usually a shiny silver colored "box" powered by a moped. It is also called BoingBoing by some Chinese, as the ride can be a bit bumpy. This is the Chinese version of the TukTuk or Moto rickshaw, which are well known all over Southeast Asia.

The fare is similar to regular taxis and should be agreed upon upfront. They can be faster in rush hour as they squeeze in between cars, use the sidewalk, opposite lanes, etc., which also makes them more dangerous than taxis.

Bicycle Rickshaws

Pedicabs or bicycle rickshaws are common in the downtown tourist areas and in the expat areas. They are great for short distances and through back streets but can feel a bit scary on bigger streets. You should negotiate the fare upfront and ideally have exact change ready. There have been a few reports of dishonest pedicab drivers.

In busy areas, like popular bar streets, all drivers seem to have agreed on a fixed fare for the vicinity, taking advantage of the fact that many women in high heels don't want to do too much walking.

Tip: Everything Western has a Chinese name and is known to most Chinese only by the Chinese name, e.g., Starbucks is Xīn bā kè 星巴克, Walmart is Wò ěr mǎ 沃尔玛. This holds true for everything that has a western name, including hotels, stores, and sights. When telling a cab driver your destination or asking for directions, make sure you know the Chinese name and its proper pronunciation or show it to him written in characters.

CARS

The easiest way of moving around is if you have a car and a driver, but it is not always the fastest or cheapest way. Driving yourself with your own car is not an immediate option for newcomers. China requires foreigners residing in China to get a Chinese driver's license, which is not that difficult. Obtaining the license plates for owning a car is the challenge, but you could still rent one or maybe get one through your company. I would advise experiencing traffic in Beijing for a while before considering driving here yourself.

CAR RENTALS IN CHINA

CAR RENTAL OVERVIEW

Despite the hectic and dense traffic, if you feel up to the task of driving and getting acquainted with the traffic laws of China, then you can rent a car from any of the local or global car rental agencies. However, there are some steps you have to follow before you can go around in your vehicle.

REQUIREMENTS TO RENT A CAR

In order to drive in China, you first need to apply for a People's Republic of China driver's license. Kindly place your international license back in your bag as they are not recognized by Chinese authorities. While applying for a Chinese license, the following are documents you will be asked to provide:

- Passport and Entry Visa
- Residence Permit valid for a period of at least 3 months
- Current Valid National Drivers License
- Certificate of physical examination for driving license application, available from public hospitals

After this is a written examination that you have to pass; this exam takes approximately 3 hours. To assist with translation and document completion, non-Chinese speakers are advised to take a bilingual interpreter with them. From here, the process is similar to those found in Western countries.

With the license obtained, you can now rent a car. China's car rental companies offer wide vehicle selections. When you arrive at the rental location:

- Present your passport, Chinese driving license, and credit card.
- Select any additional insurances required.
- Provide your verification documents and leave a deposit upwards of 5500 RMB.
- Go through and sign your Rental Agreement

In order to protect their interests many agencies require customers to undergo a lengthy process of document verification or to provide a local guarantor before allowing a foreigner to rent a car, so be prepared to do so.

HIRING A PERSONAL DRIVER

Most foreigners prefer to rent a car with a personal driver. This is understandable because of lack of understanding of the terrain by foreigners as well as other issues. The option of hiring a personal driver is readily available, reasonably priced, and can be rented long-term.

The process of renting a chauffeur-driven vehicle is easy. Chauffeur-driven vehicles are usually reserved for half or full day rentals. Although the rates are a bit high, when all the costs are considered, the prices are justified.

TAKING A BUS IN CHINA

For whatever reason, you can ditch the planes and trains and simply travel by bus. China's massive intercity bus system is often your best bet when trying to get around.

Bus Transportation

There are a number of reasons you might want to take a bus in China, but there are a few cons to also. The experience can be pleasurable and not so pleasurable while traveling in a bus. Let's take a look at a few pros of taking the bus.

Frequency: Chinese buses do run at a higher frequency than flights and trains in China. You don't have to book in advance considering there are buses running between cities every 20 minutes.

Convenience: Compared to Chinese airports and train stations, security at a bus station is not as stringent. All you need do is to arrive at the bus station a short period before departure, 30 minutes is best.

Location: Chinese bus stations are mostly located in the heart of the city as opposed to airports and train stations, which are usually on the outskirts of town. This not only saves time, but it also saves you the expense of taking a taxi far out of town.

Availability of tickets: You can always purchase a ticket on the day of departure, which you can't do when using a plane or a train. Unlike flight and train tickets, China bus tickets tend to have more availability, giving you the flexibility to change your itinerary at a moment's notice.

Now that we have looked at some pros, here are some reasons why bus travel in China may not be so pleasurable:

Unreliable Comfort: It's always a game of luck when it comes to the kind of vehicle you get to ride in, sometimes the bus is relatively new, but in most cases, you get to ride in an old vehicle. It's a risk you take, and sometimes it can be quite uncomfortable.

Delays: No matter what form of transportation you decide to take, unexpected delays are bound to happen. Buses usually leave right on time, but there arises the unpredictability of the roads, city traffic, security checkpoints or road construction. Be aware that this form of transportation could lead to delays in getting to your destination.

Fellow passengers: Riding a bus is the common man's (poor man) form of transportation. So it's usually crowded, noisy, and disorderly. The rules are much more relaxed in Chinese buses, so you might have to sit next to someone with a hen or far worse. You get to see all sorts of characters, which might annoy you and make you regret taking the bus.

Despite this, taking the bus is kind of an initiation phase in getting welcome to China, just don't expect too much out of it.

INSIDE A CHINESE BUS

There are two basic kinds of buses in China: the seated and the sleeper bus.

Seated Bus: In this type of bus, there are usually two sets of two seats with a middle aisle. All of the seats in this type of bus will be facing toward the front of the bus. The seats do recline slightly and tend to be narrow.

Most buses have an entertainment system that plays Chinese movies throughout the duration of the journey and some tend to have an air-conditioning and heating system. A few seated buses have a bathroom, but these are often not suitable for use… I learned this the hard way. All seats on a seatod bus are priced equally and these prices are fixed.

Sleeper Bus: A sleeper bus is quite different from the seated bus; rather than having seats, each traveler has a bed. There are usually three rows of beds with two aisles in between and a bathroom towards the back. Each bed has a top and bottom that runs the entire length of the bus. These buses usually have entertainment, air conditioning, and heating systems. The top bunk costs more than the bottom bunk on a sleeper bus.

GETTING TO A CHINESE BUS STATION

Most cities in China have a number of different bus stations. Often, bus stations are categorized by which direction the buses are headed (north, south, east or west) or even by which specific city. You need to know exactly which bus station you want to go to. If in doubt, you could use the following means:

Travel Guide Books or Websites: Detailed information is usually given on which bus stations to go to in different cities in the best China travel guide books or websites.

Ask Your Hotel: Even if they don't have an idea, they'll be able to ask the appropriate people and then write down the name of the bus station on a piece of paper that you can hand your taxi driver, or even offer taxi services that could take you to the exact bus station.

Ask Your Taxi Driver: Don't just tell the taxi driver to head to a bus station, tell him specifically which city you're taking a bus to. Most times, the taxi driver will know where you should go.

HOW TO BUY BUS TICKETS IN CHINA

The option of buying bus tickets online isn't currently available, so you're left with either buying a ticket at the bus station or having someone buy it for you.

China runs on a "real-name ticket system," this means that you need an official form of ID (your passport) in order to purchase bus tickets. Once your ticket is bought, you can't transfer the ticket to anybody else without returning it and buying a new one.

You need to arrive on the day of departure, stand in line, and purchase a ticket. It's important to use cash when purchasing bus tickets as foreign bank cards usually are not accepted.

TWO-WHEELERS LIKE BIKES AND SCOOTERS

Bikes are not as common anymore as they used to be, but you still see similar tendencies. In addition to the old-fashioned human-propelled version, there are electric bikes, small scooters that look like a small moped but are usually battery-run, and more regular-size scooters that can be electrical or gas powered. Real motorcycles, however, are not common.

There are quite a few of startups "Uber for bikes" such as Ofo or Mobike, where yellow, blue or orange bikes can be rented on demand and paid for with a Smartphone app once the user has arrived at their destination and parked the bike.

From what I understand, you don't need a license for a scooter, making them a favorite choice among foreigners. Wearing a helmet is not required and you won't see many people taking that safety precaution.

Many neighborhoods have bike lanes, but those must be shared with small motorized vehicles, including Sanlunches, pedestrians venturing into the street, and the occasional parked car – so watch out!

WALK

Last but not least, the most common form of "transportation" is your own feet. Be prepared to walk a lot, especially if you rely on public transportation. Distances are often huge, even changing subway lines at some intersections requires several minutes of walking. Comfortable shoes are a must in Beijing. Also keep in mind that the city is often quite dusty and some areas are not very clean, so not really a place for expensive shoes.

HIGH SPEED TRAINS IN CHINA

China currently boasts having the longest high-speed network in the world. High-speed rail services were introduced in April 2007. The trains are similar to French TGV, German ICE, and Japanese Shinkansen.

High-speed Train

This is easily the best way of getting around China where available. These trains are neat, comfortable, and modern. Seating is similar to what you would find on an airplane or even better. Unlike other trains, no smoking is allowed, not even between carriages. Prices are reasonable by western standards and, on most routes, departures are frequent.

Although China has a well developed and advanced airport infrastructure, the country suffers from serious flight delays whereas the high-speed rail network is very punctual. Although the flight from Beijing to Shanghai (for example) is shorter than the train ride, once you take travel time to/from the airport and the likelihood of long delays into account, the rail connection is far more appealing.

The fast trains are called CRH, China Railway High-speed. At some train stations there is a separate CRH ticket office or even vending machines; at others, CRH tickets are sold at separate counters in the main ticket office. In either case, just look for the "CRH" signs or logo.

Below are the top 10 fastest train trips in China, i.e., the fastest trains by average trip speed. Prices provided are approximate.

1. BEIJING–SHANGHAI HSR — FASTEST TRIP

- Distance: 1,318 km (819 mi)
- Duration: 4 h and 48 min; if by air: 2 h 10 min
- Average speed: 299 kph (186 mph)
- Price for a second class seat: 553 yuan (83 USD); a flight ticket: 1,200 yuan (193 USD)

This railway line has a north–south trend. Departing from Beijing, you will cross the two longest rivers in China — the Yellow River and the Yangtze River — then arrive in Shanghai.

See Beijing–Shanghai High-Speed Trains for the timetable and prices.

Recommended tour: Prince William's Footprint: Beijing and Shanghai via Bullet Train

2. BEIJING–SHENZHEN HSR — THE LONGEST IN THE WORLD

- Distance: 2,203 km (1,369 mi)

- Duration: 8 h; if by air: 3½ h
- Average speed: 275 kph (171 mph)
- Price for a second class seat: 936.5 (141 USD); a flight ticket: 2,000 yuan (301 USD)

This train route is part of the longest high-speed railway network in the world. The Shenzhen to Hong Kong section is not open yet. It connects North China, Central China, and South China so the landscapes on the way change every hour.

Although 8 hours on a train is quite a long time, it's a good choice to save money on your China trip. It's also a special experience to take a train traveling more than 2,200 km (1,367 mi) in distance.

Recommended tour: Window of the World, the second highest building in China (Ping An Finance Center)

3. SHANGHAI–NANJING HSR — LINKING THE YANGTZE DELTA CITIES

- Distance: 301 km (187 mi)
- Duration: 1 h 7 min; if by air: 1 h 5 min; if by bus: 4 h
- Average Speed: 268.75 kph (167 mph)
- Price for a second class seat: 139.5 yuan (22 USD); a flight ticket: 410 yuan (62 USD); a bus ticket: 88 yuan (13 USD)

Shanghai and Nanjing are two neighboring cities, and the journey duration is about 1 hour. Hangzhou and Suzhou are also within the 1-hour high-speed train route network. You can travel between these four cities conveniently.

See Shanghai – Nanjing High-Speed Trains for the timetable and prices.

Recommended tour: 5-Day Shanghai, Hangzhou, and Suzhou Bullet Train Tour.

4. WUHAN–GUANGZHOU HSR — LINKING CANTON WITH CENTRAL CHINA

- Distance: 968 km (601 mi)
- Duration: 3 h 39 min; if by air: 1 h 40 min
- Average speed: 265.2 kph (165 mph)
- Price for a second class seat: 463.5 yuan (75 USD); a flight ticket: 900 yuan (145 USD)
- Hubu AlleyHubu Alley Snack Street

This train mostly goes through hills and the main feature of this train route is that there are many bridges.

5. HARBIN–DALIAN HSR

- Distance: 904 km (562 mi)
- Duration: 3½ h; if by air: 1 h 45 min
- Average speed: 258.3 kph (161 mph)
- Price for a second class seat: 403.5 (65 USD); a flight ticket: 620 yuan (100 USD)

This is the first high-speed railway line in Northeast China. It's convenient for passengers (from Japan and Korea) who are taking an international cruise at Dalian Port.

Recommended tour: 1-Day Ice and Snow Fairyland Tour in Winter

6. GUANGZHOU–SHENZHEN HSR — THE FASTEST PEARL RIVER DELTA TRANSPORT

- Distance: 116 km (72 mi)
- Duration: 29 minutes; if by bus: 2 h
- Average speed: 242 kph (150 mph)
- Price for a second class seat: 74.5 yuan (11 USD); a bus ticket: 60 yuan (9 USD)

Guangzhou Chimelong Safari Park Guangzhou Chimelong Safari Park

Guangzhou–Shenzhen railway line connects these two popular cities in South China. These two cities also have convenient train and bus routes to Hong Kong.

7. THE SHANGHAI MAGLEV — CENTRAL SHANGHAI TO PUDONG AIRPORT IN 8 MINUTES!

- Distance: 30 km (19 mi)
- Duration: 8 min; if by taxi: 35 min
- Average speed: 230 kph (143 mph)
- Price for a single trip ticket: 50 yuan (8 USD); taxi fare: 120 yuan (19 USD)

As the length of the Shanghai Maglev track is only 30 kilometers, the average speed of Shanghai Maglev trains is only 230 kph (143 mph). It's very convenient for passengers who need to catch a flight to Shanghai Pudong International Airport.

As the first magnetically levitated train service in the world, these trains don't have wheels!

Recommended tour: 3-Day Essence of Shanghai and Watertown Tour.

8. ZHENGZHOU–XI'AN HSR — QUICK TRANSPORTATION AROUND THE ANCIENT CHINA CORRIDOR

- Distance: 455 km (283 mi)
- Duration: 2 h 4 min; no direct flight.
- Average speed: 227 kph (141 mph)
- Price for a second class seat: 239 yuan (38 USD)

This railway connects Central China and West China. It's also part of the west–east route connecting East China and Northwest China.

Recommended tour: 2-Day Essence of Xi'an Tour

9. BEIJING–HARBIN HSR — AN EXCELLENT WINTER TOURISM OPTION

- Distance: 1,700 km (1,056 mi)
- Duration: 7 h 52 min; if by air: 1 h 55 min
- Average speed: 216 kph (134 mph)
- Price for a second class seat: 541 yuan (87 USD); a flight ticket: 1,088 yuan (175 USD)

This high-speed railway is very popular for travelers in the winter. People go to Harbin to enjoy the ice and snow world attraction, skiing, and the ice sculpture festival.

Recommended tour: 4-Day Harbin Ice Wonderland and Short Ski Tour

10. BEIJING–TIANJIN INTERCITY HSR — BEST CRUISE TO CAPITAL TRANSPORT

- Distance: 115 km (71 mi)
- Duration: 33 min; if by bus: 1 h 30 min
- Average Speed: 209 kph (130 mph)
- Price for a second class seat: 65.5 yuan (10 USD); a bus ticket: 60 yuan (9 USD)

This train route is very convenient for travelers taking an international cruise out of Tianjin Port. Compared to a bus journey, which takes about 2½ hours, a high-speed train is much more convenient.

Recommended tour: 2-Day Beijing Boutique Tour

Slow Speed trains in China

While they are far less comfortable, slow speed trains are much cheaper. For example, I took an overnight train from Kunming to Dali with a soft sleeper. As we were four friends, a closed compartment was quite private, the comfort in the train was minimal, cleanliness as well. No toilet paper in the toilet, common areas were quite crowded. The train arrived at the final station 40 minutes early, but it took us a while to understand it as all announcements were made in Chinese only. However, this was an interesting experience anyway.

LOCAL FLIGHTS IN CHINA

Local Chinese flights offer great services, not only are the planes very neat and in most cases new, but the problem of the language barrier is minimal, as there is always a staff member that can communicate to you in English.

The one major concern when traveling by air within China is the crowd, this is because it gets very busy at local airports and it can take a while to get through check-in and security.

Flight tickets can be purchased via travel agents, at your hotel, at airline offices, via the airline website, or via online flight aggregator websites. Of course, the prices vary for flights and can be based on demand, but generally the earlier you book, the cheaper the flights will be.

Many hotels and accommodation facilities for tourists offer flight and tour booking services, but most will also charge a small commission for this additional service. This is definitely the easiest option for most people. You may also check with local travel agents who often have desks/offices in shopping malls, supermarkets, etc.

Airlines also have local offices where you can book tickets. A convenient option is the online booking system found on most Chinese airlines' websites; they may also have a telephone booking system that is only a call away.

Another option is to book online via the various discount flight aggregator websites. On these sites, you can check for the best deals and flight times from various airlines. When booking a flight, there is an 'e-ticket' option, which allows you to just show your passport at check-in, pick up a hard copy of the ticket at a nearby agent or have a hard copy of the ticket delivered to your location.

ONLINE FLIGHT BOOKING SERVICES

http://www.ctrip.com

http://www.elong.net

http://www.qunar.com(chinese)

LIST OF CHINA'S DOMESTIC AIRLINES

http://www.shenzhenair.com

http://www.hnair.com/ (flies to Australia)

http://www.airchina.com

http://www.shandongair.com.cn

http://www.csair.com

http://www.shanghai-air.com

http://www.xiamenair.com.cn/

http://www.dragonair.com / http://www.cathaypacific.com (flies to Australia)

(Servicing these Chinese airports: Beijing, Shanghai, Changsha, Chengdu, Chongqing, Dalian, Fuzhou, Guangzhou, Hangzhou, Hong Kong, Kunming, Nanjing, Ningbo, Qigdao, Sanya, Wuhan, Xiamen)

http://en.airmacau.com.mo/

(Servicing these Chinese airports: Shanghai, Beijing, Xiamen, Nanjing, Shenzhen, Changsha, Chengdu, Guilin, Haikou, Kunming, Hangzhou)

TOP HOTELS IN CHINA

Beautiful Hotel Accommodations

Whatever your reason for traveling to China, be it for business or pleasure, here are some of the best hotels that you could consider staying at:

1.   *AMANFAYUN*

This is a luxury resort and hotel located in Hangzhou. It is beautifully designed like a traditional Chinese village, housed in a complex of buildings. The hotel is surrounded by tea fields, forests filled with wooded bamboo, tree-lined avenues and temples. These sceneries give the hotel an extraordinary look.

Amanfayun has 47 buildings that are all over 100 years old. Upgraded with adequate facilities, the various amenities like the cigar room, library, lounge, spa, and tea room will make your stay a pleasurable one.

2. JING'S RESIDENCE

This hotel is located in the walled city of Pingyao. The first thought you have when you catch a glimpse of Jing's residence is that it belongs in an ancient Chinese movie. The hotel was originally a courtyard home of a rich merchant. Although it's small (only 19 rooms), it's one of the most luxurious accommodations you will find in China.

One of the major attractions is the excellent finish. For example, it has a rice paper ceiling and carved wooden window frames that make the hotel look very elegant. Jing's residence is a member of Relais and Chateaux, an exclusive collection of the finest hotels and most exclusive restaurants around the world.

3. GRAND HYATT, SHANGHAI

This is the highest hotel in the world. It is located in the heart of Pudong, Shanghai's business district, on the 53rd to 87th floors of the Jin Mao Tower. It offers 555 rooms and suites with floor-to-ceiling windows and provides breathtaking views of the city.

4. KEMPINSKI HOTEL, CHENGDU

This is a unique hotel that provides a great blend of European hospitality and contemporary Chinese style. Its location (in Chengdu) makes it ideal for anyone visiting China for business or pleasure. If you are in the country for pleasure, you can visit several UNESCO World Heritage-designated natural wonders that are very close to the hotel.

5.   GRACE, BEIJING

Located in the 798 Art District of Beijing, this hotel combines the buzz of the Chinese capital and the highest standards of an award-winning boutique hotel group. Attention to detail is the signature of this group; it prevails here as well. If you want to find a cozy home in the district of art, fashion, and creativity, and grace, then Beijing is for you.

6.   AMAN at SUMMER PALACE, BEIJING

Located just steps from the famous Summer Palace, this hotel captures the main features of the Ming Dynasty's elegant aesthetic. The Aman at Summer Palace blends itself into both the past and the present of China, surrounding you with calmness and serenity in the busy capital of Beijing.

7.   PARK HYATT HOTEL, BEIJING

This hotel is located in the heart of Beijing's Central Business District; it is the tallest skyscraper on Chang Avenue and a symbol of the dynamic modern China. Directly opposite China's World Trade Centre and the new CCTV Tower, this 5-star luxury hotel is less than an hour from the Beijing Capital International Airport. Park Hyatt

Beijing offers gracious service and contemporary accommodation.

8. CHINA WORLD HOTEL

Located in the heart of Beijing's political and commercial area, this hotel is well received by the majority of visitors. It has a total of 745 rooms and luxury suites; in-room modern facilities are readily available, including a luxury desk, international direct dial telephone, and satellite broadcasters. Every morning, the guests staying at the hotel can enjoy breakfast in the hotel's restaurants and can take part in a variety of activities. Guests can also enjoy the sauna, steam bath, and partake in a professional massage.

9. BEIJING KERRY CENTER HOTEL

Located in the central business district, this makes for a very convenient transportation. There are 487 guest rooms and suites, with each room having a well-designed desk, color TV, private safe, refrigerator, mini-bar, private bathroom and so on. In addition, there are several noteworthy restaurants in the hotel, including Horizon. The Horizon gives guests exclusive VIP-style service.

10. BEIJING INTERNATIONAL HOTEL

Beijing International Hotel

This is a five-star hotel located in the central area of foreign affairs and business. The hotel style speaks of simple luxury, elegance, and brilliance as a whole, displaying the different aspects of Western and Eastern civilization. The 1049 well-appointed guestrooms and suites are equipped with central air-conditioning control system, mini bar, refrigerator, electronic locks, and international direct dial telephone. The hotel also has a convenient and quiet environment, all of which make it the first choice for people spending their holidays in Beijing.

5 BEST HOTELS ON BUDGET IN BEIJING

Beijing's budget hotels have a lot to offer. These options will offer you a safe, cheap place to rest your head without compromising on the basic essentials. These hotel options are in decent locations in and around Beijing. You'll easily find restaurants, bars or top tourist sites near the hotels. After all, you're in Beijing to see the attractions, not to see the interior of your hotel, so pick a place that is located in a cool area and you won't regret it.

Budget hotels in China are not like motels and cheap hotels in Europe and America. Most budget hotels in China are used for traveling businessmen, as local families don't usually go on road trips or vacations where they need to stay in a hotel. Thus, most hotels will be full of men in suits who are smoking, drinking, and enjoying the lifestyle. For this reason, most hotels smell of smoke. Also, the breakfast room will be empty after 9 a.m. because most businessmen will be off doing their trade.

1. JIADEJIA EXPRESS HOTEL

This simple and small hotel offers a few amenities, but the real draw is it's central location around a fun, local area where you'll be able to immerse yourself into the community quickly and easily. Local restaurants and a few simple dive bars complete the picture of a classic Beijing community. The rooms are decent, as is the service, and you'll be provided with a hard, but comfortable bed with clean bedding and towels. A private bathroom offers a shower with hot water available usually 24 hours a day. Air conditioning provided in some, but not all rooms so check before you book your room.

2. MOTEL 168

This massive Chinese chain offers a decent stay. You'll find a small in-house restaurant that offers a cheap breakfast option offering eggs, rice, and usually a vegetable or two. I'd advise skipping the breakfast in favor of Starbucks nearby, but that's just a suggestion. The hotel rooms have a simple bed, usually quite hard as is the Chinese way, and bedding. Towels and access to a bathroom (sometimes shared, but usually private) are also included. The phone, TV, and air-conditioning are all provided in most rooms, though consider clarifying before you book the room.

3. REST MOTEL

Feel confident knowing that Rest Motel is a place where you'll find everything you need and more for an enjoyable stay in the capital of the Middle Kingdom. Simple digs include a bed, bedding, towels, access to a bathroom and, of course, the all-important hotel TV and phone. At low-end places, the phone is primarily a tool for the local "massage parlor" to call your room to offer full body massages. An in-house restaurant offers a simple breakfast for those in a rush, and with other restaurants nearby you will not go hungry around the dinner hour either.

4.   GUOHAN HOTEL

Guohan Hotel is a simple place to rest after a long day of sightseeing and adventures. Rest assured, you'll have everything you need and more at this hotel. Towels, a decent bathroom, bedding, and a few features like a phone, TV, and air conditioning make this a great place to stay on a tight budget. Don't overanalyze the simple decor and less-than-elegant service, this place specializes in simplicity and function - exactly what the budget traveler ordered. A simple breakfast is on hand, and with restaurant and bar options nearby you'll be able to easily find food or entertainment.

5.   ADEN HOTEL

This simple hotel offers everything you'd need for a short stay in Beijing without breaking the bank. Accommodations include a simple bed, and in most cases, two twin beds for businessmen traveling together. A phone, TV, and a few other simple features complete the room. Don't be put off by the dingy decor and cheap, plastic plants. The rooms are comfortable and clean, and that's all you need for a budget stay in Beijing. If you want high-end decor head to the Four Seasons, but be prepared to pay a small fortune for better service, decor, and amenities. At Aden, the real focus is on function.

RENTING AN APARTMENT IN BEIJING

You may find yourself traveling halfway around the world to Beijing without knowing what your next home looks like. Freaking out at the idea of searching frantically for an apartment while staying in a hotel? Understandable. But don't worry. Finding and leasing a flat in Beijing can be pretty easy.

WHEN SHOULD YOU START LOOKING FOR AN APARTMENT IN BEIJING?

Many people want to have a nice place to live lined up when they move to a new location. You could try to do this and find a home in Beijing online with the help of real estate agents. But this is not really necessary.

I would say it is not even advisable. You could be in for a huge surprise when renting something unseen without visiting the neighborhood and actually seeing the apartment and the building.

Beijing rentals are usually available for immediate move-in, so it doesn't make much sense to look too far out in advance.

HOW MUCH DOES RENT COST IN BEIJING?

Apartments in Beijing are expensive, compared to other costs of living here. For example, 2-3 bedroom flats in an expat-friendly residential compound with some western amenities can easily cost 20,000 RMB or more a month (as of mid 2015).

At the lower end, expect to pay 7,000 RMB and up for a small 2 bedroom place in an older Chinese compound. Less if you are willing to live further outside the city. You won't find many western amenities in this price range.

If this is still too much, a room in a shared flat starts at around 3000 RMB.

Please keep in mind that the surface is calculated in "Chinese meters," so in usual terms the apartment would be smaller - Chinese include walls, balconies, staircase, etc., into those measurements.

MORE ABOUT LEASE TERMS AND FEES

Apartments in Beijing are usually offered with 6 or 12-month lease terms, sometimes even longer. Rent is paid in advance in 3 or 6 month increments.

In addition to rent, the landlord usually requires a refundable deposit of 1 month's rent. I've heard stories from some people who have had difficulty getting their deposit returned when they moved out.

Usually apartments are rented through the help of a real estate agent. The agent is paid a fee equivalent to 1 month's rent. The amount can be negotiable though.

HOW TO FIND AN APARTMENT IN BEIJING?

An evening in Beijing

You can enlist multiple agents to help you find the right apartment for you. Once you have narrowed down the area or even the compound where you want to live, you can look for agents there. They are easy to spot, often outside with signs in front of a real estate office.

One challenge though is that most agents don't speak much English. So you will need the help of a Chinese-speaking friend or colleague. You can also ask around for recommendations for English-speaking agents.

Be prepared for agents to show you a lot of apartments, including crappy ones and ones above your price range. Be firm with what you are looking for.

If you are only looking for a room in a shared flat, you can sometimes avoid agents. Look at the classifieds section of The Beijinger website. The ads posted by agents are easy to spot. Private posts clearly say "No agent fee."

In general, if you look at apartment ads from agents online, be aware that photos are often not real and show a different place than the one advertised. Often the bathroom or kitchen are not shown at all. When you contact the agent, he or she may not know which property you are referring to and may try to show you other apartments instead.

The easiest way to communicate with agents and everyone else here is via WeChat, a Chinese messaging app similar to WhatsApp but better. You can easily delete or block contacts that you don't want anymore. It is also a great tool for requesting more photos before you invest the time to go and see a place.

The most helpful real estate agencies I have used were **Real Scout agency** and **CityWise**. Also, you can consult with some useful websites like www.thebeijinger.com, www.expatarrivals.com, www.beijingexpatguide.com. The best compounds to live for Expats would be Soho Sanlitun, Beijing Golf Palace, Park Appartments, and Central Park.

WESTERN SHOPS, MARKETS IN BEIJING

Shopping is an important aspect of our everyday lives, whether for basic daily necessities, luxury items, retail therapy or just window shopping. One of the fun activities one can engage in while in other countries is to check out what is being sold and how these items are being sold.

Below are some of the expectations when going shopping in Beijing.

GROCERIES

In Beijing, supermarkets are everywhere. The Chinese chains, Chaoshifa and Jinkelong can be found all over the city. Their stores carry fresh produce, meat, dairy products, alcohol, and all kind of stuff you would expect in a supermarket, but not necessarily typical western products.

The BHG supermarkets on the other hand provide a wide range of western products and produce. These supermarkets are usually located in the basement of big shopping malls, the likes of the Hualian & Capital Mall. China also has western supermarket chains like the American Walmart (Chinese name: wó ěr mǎ 沃尔玛) and even French chains, Carrefour (jiā lè fú 家乐福) and Auchan. Even with these options, the selection can be limited and expensive.

The major western supermarkets are Jenny Lou's and April Gourmet. These chains carry imported food, have fresh western bread, fresh produce, some imported personal care items, and much more. They are found in the Eastern part of Beijing in Chaoyang and Shunyi. A new western supermarket has opened in Haidian district of Wudaokou. It is located inside the Huaqing Jiajuan, west of the subway station.

FRESH PRODUCTS

Most supermarkets sell fresh produce, but the freshest and cheapest can actually be found in fresh markets such as farmers markets and roadside markets. These markets tend to be a bit hidden in-between residential buildings. To locate these markets, you have to be observant; just look around for people carrying enormous amounts of veggies in plastic bags or in a "bag on wheels" and see where they are coming from.

One of the advantages of these markets is that you get to bargain the price. These markets are geared towards the Chinese household and only sell what is commonly used in cooking Chinese meals.

Looking for more western ingredients, the Sanyuanli market in the Sanlitun area specializes in non-Chinese produce geared towards foreigners and therefore the vendors also speak some English. At this market, you can find brussel sprouts, basil, even Thai basil if you are lucky, lemon grass, kaffir lime leaves, and other non-Chinese vegetables. Even the chefs of indigenous restaurants come here.

There is also a little Indian supermarket called Qi Yuan Market right behind the Sanlitun Village and Yashow market, across from the police station, which carries Indian spices and food items.

If you are looking for organic produce, check out the Beijing Organic Farmers Market. There are also organic farms from which you can order online and get the food delivered to your home.

CLOTHING

Buying clothes is usually an essential part of one's agenda, whether as a necessity or just for the fun of it. In Beijing, western-style shopping malls with numerous clothing stores are very popular and located in most neighborhoods. They always offer a mix of Chinese and international brands.

Haggling is not allowed at shopping malls, but the stores often have sales going on. The shopping malls often have a supermarket and a food court in the basement and restaurants on the top levels.

It is important to note that the prices of foreign chain stores are often higher than what is obtainable in the US or Europe. You can also find smaller clothing stores on the street, sometimes just a rack of clothings or a table that displays socks or shirts, etc.; bargaining is possible here. Foreigners can also shop for clothes at the Silk and Pearl markets.

HOUSEHOLD ITEMS

Walmart, Carrefour, and other bigger supermarkets and departmental stores in shopping malls are stores were appliances and other household items can be bought. These household items can also be bought at local electronic stores like Suning or through online sites.

If you need furniture or decorative items there is always IKEA (Yí jiā 宜家), which is situated northeast just outside

the fourth ring road. They deliver to your doorstep, but keep in mind you have to give your exact location in Chinese. Also, if the items are not too big and can fit in a small car, there are taxis available at the exit. Other furniture stores can also be found on the northeast fourth ring road.

CHINESE RESTAURANTS

Famous Chinese restaurants in major cities in China are top choices for anyone who wants to get the best out of Chinese cuisines. The handpicked restaurants below are the most famous and historic ones in China.

1.   QUANJUDE — PEKING DUCK

Chinese: 全聚德 Quánjùdé /chwen-jyoo-der/

Specializing in Peking duck, Quanjude (/chwen-jyoo-der/) started their business in Beijing back in the Qing Dynasty (1864). It has now become a household name for Beijing roast duck, a must-taste food in Beijing and China.

Beijing Branches:

•   The biggest roasted duck restaurant in the world — Hepingmen Branch: Building 14, Qianmen West Street, Xuanwu District (宣武区前门西大街 14 号楼)

•   The original Quanjude restaurant — Qianmen Branch: 32 Qianmen Street, Chongwen District (崇文区前门大街 32 号)

• Wangfujing Branch: 9 Shuaifuyuan Hutong, Dongcheng District (东城区帅府园胡同 9 号)

Shanghai Branches:

• Zhabei Branch: 547 Tianmu West Road, Zhabei District (天目西路 547 号)

• Pudong Branch: Floor 3, Zijinshan Hotel, 778 Dongfang Road, Pudong New District (浦东新区东方路 778 号紫金山大酒店 3 楼)

2.　*SOUTH BEAUTY — SICHUAN CUISINE*

Chinese: 俏江南 Qiàojiāngnán /chyaoww-jyang-nan/

South Beauty has its headquarters in Beijing. It also has three high-rate affiliate brands: South Beauty Restaurant, LAN Club, and SUBU. Although it started doing business in 2000, South Beauty now has more than 50 branches across China. They specialize in serving up a combination of elegant environment and delicious Chinese dishes.

Beijing Branches:

• Guomao Center Branch: L220, (second floor) Guomao Mansion West Building, 1 Jianguomenwai Street, Chaoyang District (朝阳区建国门外大街 1 号国贸大厦西楼 2 楼 L220 号)

- Xidan Branch: 7-1, 7 Huayuan Street, Xicheng District (西城区华远街 7 号楼 7-1)

Shanghai Branches

- Xintiandi Branch: Units 2 & 5, 235 Xintiandi Beili, 181 Alley, Taicang Road, Luwan District (卢湾区太仓路181弄新天地北里235号02、05单元)

- Global Financial Center Branch: Room 307, (third floor) Global Financial Center, 100 Century Avenue, Pudong New District (浦东新区世纪大道100号环球金融中心3楼307室)

- Zhongshan Park Branch: Floor 8, Longzhimeng, 1088 Changning Road, Changning District (长宁区长宁路1088号龙之梦8楼)

Guangzhou Branches:

- Tianhecheng Branch: 703A–704, 208 Tianhecheng Road, Tianhe District (天河区天河城路208号703A至704

3. *HAIDILAO — HOTPOT*

Chinese: 海底捞 Hǎidǐlāo /heye-dee-laow/

Business for Haidilao began in 1994, and since then they have opened branches in 15 cities across China. Their specialty is in Sichuan hotpot.

Beijing Branches:

- Wangfujing Branch: Floor 8, Letian Yintai Shopping Mall, 88 Wangfujing Shopping Street, Dongcheng District (东城区王府井大街88号乐天银泰百货8楼)

- Xidan Branch: Floor 7, Xidan Hunqing Building, 109 Xidan North Avenue, Xicheng District (西城区西单北大街109号西单婚庆大楼7楼)

Shanghai Branches:

• Zhangyang Road Branch: Floor 6, Bainaohui, 588 Zhangyang Road, Pudong New District (浦东新区张杨路588 号百脑汇 6 楼)

• Xujiahui Branch: Floor 5, Bailian Xuhui Commercial Plaza South, 2068 Huashan Road, Xuhui District (徐汇区华山路 2068 号百联徐汇商业广场南 5 楼)

4.   *MORALS VILLAGE — HOTPOT*

Chinese: 德庄火锅 Dézhuāng Huǒguō /der-jwung hwor-gwor/

Morals Village's hotpot is one of the most famous brands of Sichuan hotpot. They specialize in making hotpots with all sorts of fresh ingredients.

Chengdu Branches:

- Yushuang Branch: 2 Yushuang Road, Chenghua District (成华区玉双路 2 号)

- Qingjiang Branch: 198 Qingjiang East Road, Qingyang District (青羊区清江东路 198 号)

Chongqing Branches:

- Majiabao Branch: 174 Changjiang Second Road, Yuzhong District (渝中区长江二路 174)

- Xuetianwan Branch: Floor 2, 55 Xuetianwan Zheng Street, Yuzhong District (渝中区学田湾正街 55 号 2 楼)

5. *SICHUAN FOLK — SICHUAN CUISINE*

Chinese: 巴国布衣 Bāguó Bùyī /baa-gwor-boo-ee/

Established in 1996, Sichuan Folk practices traditional hotpot culture. However, it has also created a new concept of Sichuan cuisine.

Chengdu Branches:

- Shenxianshu Branch: 63 Shenxianshu South Road, Wuhou District (成都武侯区神仙树南路63号)

Beijing Branches:

- Guomao Branch: Floor 2, South Airline Hotel, 10 Middle Road, East Third Ring, Chaoyang District (朝阳区东三环中路10号南航大酒店2楼)

- Xizhimen Branch: 68 Xizhimen South Small Street, Xicheng District (西城区西直门南小街68号).

Shanghai Branches:

- Pudong Branch: Floor 3, Yu'an Building, 738 Dongfang Road, Century Avenue, Pudong New District (上海浦东新区-世纪大道东方路738号裕安大厦3楼)

- Dingxi Branch: 1018 Dingxi Road, Changning District (长宁区定西路1018号)

6.   AUTHENTIC GUANGZHOU FOOD

Chinese: 广州酒家 Guǎngzhōu Jiǔjiā /gwung-joh jyoh-jyaa/

Authentic Guangzhou happens to be one of the most famous and traditional restaurants in Guangzhou. Customers never fail to say that this restaurant is the most visited restaurant in Guangzhou; its authentic Guangzhou food and snacks are very popular amongst customers.

Guangzhou Branches:

- Tianhe Branch: Floors 3 and 4, Baifu Square, 116–118 Tianhe East Road, Tianhe District (天河区体育东路116-118号百福广场3-4楼)

- Wenchang Branch: 2 Wenchang South Road, Liwan District (荔湾区文昌南路2号).

7.   *LIANXIANG LOU — MOON CAKE*

Chinese: 莲香楼 Liánxiānglóu /lyen-sshyang-loh/

In 1889, the first restaurant of Lianxiang Lou was opened in the west of Guangzhou city. Their specialty is their traditional moon cakes made with authentic lotus paste.

- Guangzhou Branch: 67 Dishifu Road, Liwan District (荔湾区第十甫路67号)

- Hong Kong Branch: 160–164 Wellington Street, Middle Ring (中环威灵顿街160-164号)

8.   *SHANGHAI OLD RESTAURANT — LOCAL SHANGHAI CUISINE*

Chinese: 上海老饭店 Shànghǎi Lǎofàndiàn /shung-heye laow-fan-dyen/

With a history dating back to the Qing Dynasty (1875), Shanghai Old Restaurant's local Shanghai cuisine dishes attract a large number of customers every year.

- Shanghai Branch: 242 Fuyou Road, Huangpu District (黄浦区福佑路242号)

- Beijing Branch: Floor 18, Zhongshang Building, 5 Sanlihe East Road, Xicheng District (西城区三里河东路5号中商大厦18楼)

9.   LVBOLANG — SHANGHAI CUISINE

Chinese: 绿波廊 Lǜbōláng /lyoo-bor-lung/

Having a history spanning over 400 years, Lvbolang is one of the famous restaurants in Shanghai.

- Shanghai Branch: 115 Yuyuan Road, City God Temple, Huangpu District (黄浦区老城隍庙内豫园路115号)
- Beijing Branch: Floor 2, Liangmahe Restaurant, 8 East Third Ring North Road, Chaoyang District (朝阳区东三环北路8号亮马河饭店2楼)

10.   LOUWAILOU — AUTHENTIC HANGZHOU DISHES

Chinese: 楼外楼 Lóuwàilóu /loh-why-loh/

With a history spanning more than 160 years, Louwailou restaurant is very famous. Located at the foot of Gushan Mountain, beside West Lake in Hangzhou, it is an excellent place to enjoy authentic Hangzhou dishes. The poetic natural scenery is also a sight to behold.

Hangzhou Branches:

- Lushan Road Branch: 30 Gushan Road, West Lake District (西湖区孤山路30号)

- Yuquan Branch: Hangzhou Plantation, 1 Taoyuanling, West Lake District (西湖区桃源岭1号杭州植物园内)

11. ZHIWEIGUAN — HANGZHOU DESSERT AND SNACKS

Chinese: 知味观 Zhīwèiguān /jrr-way-gwan/

This restaurant is situated east of busy Yan'an Road, and west of beautiful West Lake. Zhiweiguan has many special and tempting snacks, and authentic Hangzhou dishes.

Hangzhou Branches:

- Headquarters: 83 Renhe Road (仁和路83号)

- Wulin Branch: Floor 1, New Yan'an Hotel, 20 Zhijietansi Alley (直戒坛寺巷20号新延安饭店1楼)

- Zhaohui Road Branch: 26 Zhaohui Road (朝晖路26号)

Shanghai Branch:

- Floor 4, Zhihui Square, 488 Wuning South Road, Jing'an District (静安区武宁南路488号智慧广场4楼)

Beijing Branch:

- 44 Xinjiekou South Avenue, Xicheng District (西城区新街口南大街44号)

12. JIASAN STEAMED STUFFED BUN RESTAURANT — SOUP DUMPLINGS

Chinese: 贾三灌汤包 Jiǎsān Guàntāngbāo /jyaa-san gwan-tung-baoww/

Jiasan is also a famous brand for "steamed soup stuffed buns." This restaurant not only offers steamed dumplings, which are their specialty, but also provides Xi'an snacks and other dishes.

- Best Xi'an Branch: Muslim Street Branch: 93 Beiyuanmen, Muslim Street, Xiyangshi, Beilin District (碑林区西羊市回民街北院门93号)

- Beijing Branch: Building 1, Baiyunguan Street, Xicheng District (西城区白云观街甲1号楼)

TOP 5 CHINESE RESTAURANTS IN BEIJING

It's rather difficult to name the best Chinese restaurants in Beijing, but this might just be a starter list, with a few of the most delicious suggestions to start off your culinary trip in the Chinese capital.

1. HUAJIA YIYUAN (HUA'S RESTAURANT)

Huajia Yiyuan Restaurant

If you are looking for a local culinary experience that satisfies both your taste and your aesthetic expectations of "real" Chinese ambience, you should not miss Hua's Restaurant. Reaching the location via a hutong might appear a bit tricky in the beginning, but it definitely adds to the whole experience. You can enjoy a variety of mouth-watering local dishes, including a well-made Peking Duck.

235 Dongzhimen Nei Dajie, Dongcheng District, Beijing 100007, China

2. *BELLAGIO CAFE (GONG TI)*

This trendy Taiwanese and Chinese restaurant has been a favorite hangout for many local and foreign foodies as well as fashionable young crowds for years. Bellagio is famous for various delicacies like their famous tofu and beef dishes, dragon beans, pork dumplings, and their wholesome spicy hot soups. But for many its main attraction is their delicious Taiwanese desserts, including not-to-miss treats like shaved ice with mango.

6 Gongti Xilu, Chaoyang District, Beijing, China

3. *LOST HEAVEN*

Inspired by the Tea-and horse-Trail that brought tea to Tibet and horses south to Yunnan, Burma, and Thailand, Lost Heaven specializes in the delights of Yunnan and Thai folk cuisine. Its elegant dark wood and ethnic inspired décor make it an attractive spot that is perfect for a romantic dinner. The menu offers a large variety of dishes to choose from, with Yunnan cuisine being a distinct favorite. The cocktails are also exciting with bold combinations of coconut, chilis, and sweet tastes.

No.23, Qian Men Dong Da Jie, Beijing, China

4.   *BEIJING DADONG, TIAN'ANMEN/WANGFUJING*

You really cannot give suggestions about Beijing restaurants and omit the King of Peking duck: Dadong Restaurant. Having won awards and distinctions for its very high quality duck, it has opened various Dadong branches in Beijing to satisfy the growing demand. The restaurant in the heart of the city in the area of Wangfujing offers a convenient location as well as an elegant ambience in which to enjoy this Chinese delicacy.

Jinbao Place, No.88 Jinbao Street, Dongcheng District, Beijing, China

5.   *LITTLE YUNNAN*

This stylish little gem is popular for its spectacular modern Chinese cuisine as well as its "Chinese café" ambience. Located in a well-preserved courtyard near Jingshan Park, Little Yunnan's is a perfect place for lunch and dinner, and for small groups or couples looking for a romantic spot. Apart from a variety of tasty spicy Yunnan delicacies, they also serve excellent home-brewed rice wine.

No. 28 East Huangchenggen Beijie, Dongcheng district, Beijing 100009, China

TOP 5 WESTERN RESTAURANTS IN BEIJING

The western food scene in Beijing has grown tremendously in the past few years. These restaurants represent some of the best, ranging in cuisine, price, and location.

1. *THE GEORG*

Located in Beijing's hutongs, the Georg is one of the hottest upscale contemporary European restaurant opened by Danish design brand Georg Jensen. Expect your money to get you good service and solid fare.

• Price range: over 500 yuan per person

• Open: 11:30am–3pm and 6pm–10:30pm, except Sundays. Call ahead to book!

• Address: 45 Dongbuyaqiao Hutong, Dongcheng District (东城区东不压桥胡同)

• Tel: 010 8408 5300

• Transportation: Get off at Shichahai Station (Line 8) or Nanluoguxiang Station (Line 6 or Line 8).

2. STUFF'D

Stuff'd Restaurant, Beijing

This is a real local favorite that is located on Beijing's Wudaoying Hutong. Stuff'd makes their own sausages, and serves a wide range of other great Western food from pizzas to salads. They also have nice cocktails, and brew their own beer.

• Price range: around 100 yuan per person

• Open: 11am–2:45pm and 6pm–10pm, except Tuesdays

• Address: 9 Jianchang Hutong, Dongcheng District (东城区箭厂胡同9号)

• Tel: 010 6407 6308

- Transportation: Get off at Andingmen Station (Line 2) or Yonghegong Station (Line 2 or Line 5).

3. PEBBLES COURTYARD

For a good Mexican option in the Lama temple neighborhood, try Pebbles Lounge. This three-story restaurant has been open for many years, and has good burritos, nachos, and tacos at reasonable prices. Their margaritas are also worth a special mention.

- Price range: around 100 yuan per person

- Open: 12pm–11pm, Daily

- Address: 74 Wudaoying Hutong, Dongcheng District (东城区五道营胡同 74 号)

- Tel: 010 8408 0767

- Transportation: Get off at Andingmen Station (Line 2) or Yonghegong Station (Line 2 or Line 5).

4. TEMPLE RESTAURANT

This has repeatedly been named one of the best western restaurants in Beijing. The restaurant has award winning chefs and is set in an exquisite setting in an ancient Tibetan temple that was only recently discovered. The restaurant (and connecting hotel) have won preservation awards. Eating out at Temple Restaurant is a great experience.

- Price range: over 500 yuan per person

• Open: 11:30am–2:30pm Monday–Friday, 10:30am–3pm Saturday–Sunday and 5:30pm–10pm Monday–Sunday. Call ahead to book!

• Address: 23 Shantan Beijie, Dongcheng District (东城区沙滩北街 23 号)

• Tel: 010 8400 2232

• Transportation: Best way to get there is a taxi, as the subway station is not yet in operation.

5.   VINEYARD CAFE, BEIJING

Located in one of the most famous hutongs in Beijing, this restaurant boasts of a cute courtyard. The thin and crispy pizza tastes good. Their roast potato skins are liked by many customers. It is a good idea to sit in the yard in autumn and have a piece of pizza together with a cup of coffee and desserts.

• Average price per person: 100–200 yuan per person

• Open: 11:30am–11pm (closed on Mondays)

• Address: 31 Wudaoying Hutong, Dongcheng District (东城区五道营胡同 31 号)

• Tel: 010-64027961

• Transportation: Take Subway Line 5, and get off at Yonghegong Station.

ORDERING FOOD IN CHINA

In China ordering food can be quite tricky; there are no English speaking staff to help most of the time or even English menus. Here are some tips and useful phrases for ordering food in China.

READING MENUS

Menu: 菜单, cài dān, /tseye-dan/

After sitting at the table in a restaurant, and the customary pot of tea has been served, the next thing which will arrive is the menu (菜单 caidan /tseye-dan/).

MENUS WITH PICTURES

One portion: 一份, Yí Fèn, /ee fnn/

You're lucky if the menu has pictures in it as this offers an easy way to order. Just point to what you want and say yi fen (一份 /ee fnn/ 'one portion').

CHINESE PHRASE WITH PINYIN AND PRONOUNCIATION

Some Chinese menus actually have English versions, especially in larger restaurants. However, it is quite normal that the English used is incorrect or full of spelling mistakes. Sometimes, the staff might not be able to speak English at all, so you will still have to point at the menu and say yi fen anyway.

HOW MANY DISHES TO ORDER

Although the Chinese custom is always to order too much to show generosity and hospitality, I would recommend you only order what you can finish to avoid wasting food. A dish per person is usually enough. If there are a number of people eating with you, try to order a range of different dishes. Soup/broth is a customary starter in China. Sweet desserts are not a tradition in China, but caramelized bananas or apples and steamed buns with condensed milk dip are available at many restaurants.

ORDERING DUMPLINGS

Chinese dumplings (饺子 jiǎozi /jyaoww-dzrr/) are an all-time favorite even amongst foreigners. Some restaurants specialize in just dumplings. Usually, about 20 to 30 is enough for a meal, 40 if you're really hungry. Dumplings are served in traditional bamboo. So, you can say yī lóng (一笼 /ee-long/ 'one tray') followed by your choice of filling to order. Fillings include pork (猪肉 zhūròu /joo-roh/), beef

(牛肉 niúròu /nyoh-roh/), cabbage (白菜 báicài /beye-tseye/) and garlic chives/leek (韭菜 jiǔcài /jyoh-tseye/).

.

FOOD DELIVERY IN BEIJING

Many foreigners in Beijing do not cook at home. Instead, they either eat out or order food from restaurants. As a result of ordering food all the time, eating healthy and balanced is not always realizable. It is, therefore, important to introduce variety into your meals and not always order from the same restaurant.

Listed below are different food delivery companies offering services in English (and Chinese). There is an availability of variety of foods, including Chinese, Asian, French, American, Mexican, Italian, and Middle Eastern food that can be delivered to you.

FOOD DELIVERY SERVICES

1. K.K.RABBIT:

• Extras: You get one free drink if your meal fee (not including service charge) is over 50 RMB.

• Delivery fee: from 15 RMB

• Operating hours: from 10:30am-10:30pm daily.

• Served areas: Guomao, Sanlitun, Solana

• Time of delivery: 40 minutes minimum

- Phone: 400 720 1717 (English speaking staff)

- Website: http://www.kkrabbit.com.cn/

- Payment method: Cash only

2.   JINSHISONG:

- Delivery fee: 15RMB within the first 3km, 5 RMB for each extra kilometer

- Minimum order: 68 RMB

- Operating hours: from 10:30am-10:30pm daily.

- Served areas: All Beijing

- Time of delivery: 40 to 60 minutes.

- Phone: 400 300 517 (English speaking staff, an additional service fee will be charged)

- Website: http://www.jinshisong.com/restaurants

- Payment method: Cash only

3.   SHERPA:

- Extras: you can add wine or beer or soft drinks to any restaurant order without a delivery fee.

- Delivery fee: this depends on your location and the restaurant you request (minimum fee is 15 RMB)

- Minimum order:

1.   100 RMB from 6 pm

2.   200 RMB from 6 pm on rainy days

• Operating hours: from 10:30am-10:30pm.

• Served areas: Chaoyang District, Dongcheng District

• Time of delivery: 45 minutes minimum

• Phone number for Beijing: 400-600-6209 (English speaking staff)

• Website:
http://www.sherpa.com.cn/index.shtml?backHome=1

• Payment method: Cash, WeChat, credit cards

RESTAURANTS HAVING THEIR OWN DELIVERY NETWORK

1.   JUICE:

• Type of food: Fresh fruit juices, fresh vegetable juices, smoothies

• Minimum order: 78 RMB

• Served areas: Central Park, CBD, Yuan Yang Tian Di, Hua Mao, Dawang Lu, Wanda Plaza, Guanghua Lu, Lan Bao, Jin Di Hua Yuan, Dongzhimen, Sanlitun, Gongti, Tuanjiehu, Maizidian, Chaoyang Park West/South, Taikang Center, Ritan Park, Dongsi Nan Bei Da Jie (Oriental Plaza, Jinbao Jie, Chaonei Xiao Jie, …), Chaoyangmen, Jianwai Soho, Shuangjing / Fulicheng,

Guang Qu Men Wai Da Jie (Pingguo Shiqu, Beijing Zhan), Lido, Wangjing, Shunyi, Yonghegong / Lama Temple, Olympic Park, Zhongguancun / Wudaokou)

• Time of delivery: 60 to 90 minutes, prearranged time for certain areas

• Website: http://www.ifjuice.com/iF_Juice/iF_Home_ru_guo_shou_y e.html

2.   ANNIE'S:

• Type of food: Italian cuisine

• Extra: selected soft drinks and beers at half prices

• Delivery fee: Free delivery between Line 5 subway (west) and the east 5th Ring Road.

• Served areas: between Line 5 subway (west) and the east 5th Ring Road. These areas include Guomao, Wangjing, Lido, Beijing Riviera, Sunshine 100, The Place, Ritan Park, Sanlitun, Chaoyang Park…

• Time of delivery: 40 minutes to 1 hour.

• Operating hours: 10:30 a.m. – 10:30 p.m.

• Website: http://www.annies.com.cn/

3.   GUNGHO:

• Type of food: Pizza, Pasta, Salad, desserts

- Delivery fee: +15 RMB fee delivery under 45 RMB

- Served areas: Shuangjing, Sanlitun, Lido, Wangjing

- Time of delivery: during peak periods 45 – 60 minutes.

- Operating hours: 11 a.m. – 11 p.m. Mon – Sun

- Website: http://www.gunghopizza.com/

4.   *ELEMENT FRESH:*

• Type of food: Salads, pasta, sandwiches, Asian sets, desserts, fresh juices, smoothies, soft drinks, wine

- Delivery fee: Minimum order 40 RMB.

• Served areas: East Beijing (Lido, Indigo, Solana, Sanlitun, Park View Green, CBD)

- Time of delivery: /

- Operating hours: 10 a.m. to 10 p.m.

- Website: http://www.elementfresh.com/

ORGANIC FOOD IN CHINA

For a few years now, expats have been talking about organic food. With the growing rate of food safety incidents in China in the last few years, it is not only expats but also more local Chinese people have become interested in organic food.

In May of each year, Biofach, the world's leading organizer of organic food and agriculture trade fairs, hosts an exhibition in Shanghai. Organic distributors, websites, farms, and manufacturers from all over China, as well as overseas, exhibit their products.

Apart from this annual organic exhibition, organic food in Shanghai can be found at large supermarkets, including Carrefour, several Farmer's markets held in Shanghai (including the bi-weekly Saturday Jiashan market), as well as through organic food delivery services.

HOME DELIVERY OF ORGANIC FOOD IN SHANGHAI

Many organic farms in Shanghai offer a weekly home delivery service based on 3/6/12 months subscriptions. You can choose one or two deliveries per week.

There is a limited choice of two to three types of vegetable baskets, and the contents change based on the growing season, so you must accept what is delivered. Some imported organic foods can also be purchased through online stores and delivered to your location in Shanghai.

SUPPLIERS

ORGANIC FARMS in SHANGHAI

- Tony's Farm www.tonysfarm.com

- Mahota Farm www.mahotafarm.com

- Biofarm www.biofarmdirect.com

- And many others

ORGANIC RESTAURANTS

- Mahota Kitchen

- Ming Tang Shanghai

- Organic Kitchen Shanghai

- Green & Safe Shanghai

ORGANIC BAKERIES

- Abendbrot

- The Freshary

ORGANIC SHOPS IN BEIJING

Too Too organic shop www.tootoo.cn

DeRunWu www.bjchano.com

Organic Farm www.vip.organicfarm.com.cn

SILK STREET PEARL MARKET BEIJING

The Silk Street Pearl Market is one place you must go visit if you ever find yourself in Beijing. It is a well-known Chinese international tourism and shopping market. While some people will reference the Silk Market and Silk Street Market, they are actually one and the same.

Silk Street Pearl Market

The market is very easy to locate as well as access. It is located at Chang'An Avenue, Chaoyang District, not far from the international CBD business area in Beijing.

Silk Street has a history of over 30 years as one of the earliest free markets with the most famous business brands. There are nearly 2,000 stalls spread over the six floors with vendors selling goods such as: silk, pearls, porcelain, tea, handicrafts, jewelry and clothes. Ruifuixiang, Neiliansheng, Tongrentang, Qianxiangyi, ShengXifu and others totaling 18 old and famous brands make Silk Street the most traditional culture featured market.

Although the market has a reputation for selling counterfeit products, it is still popular among those looking to buy counterfeit luxury designer items. In recent times, the mall has undergone some changes and now features more high value items.

Do not forget to bargain prices. Surprisingly, the first price you get quoted can actually be more than what you would get in the U.S. or Europe, so try to beat the price to half. The trick to haggling is to always be good humored, ignore the stall owner when they act dissatisfied with your bargain; just keep on smiling, haggling, and walking away. Why? Because it is when you walk away that they will most often become more agreeable.

The big attraction here is variety, all in one place. Your bargaining skills will determine the success of this shopping spree. If you enjoy shopping, you could easily spend half a day here.

You can purchase a broad range of items from silk, jewelry, cosmetics, household goods, fashionable clothes, watches, office supplies, electronic goods, and so much more.

Opening hours: 9:30 p.m. (21:30)

How to get there: About 200 meters away from Metro Line 2, Jianguomen Station.

Address: No. 8, Xiushui East Street, Chaoyang District.

TEA STREET IN BEIJING

If you're a huge fan of Chinese movies, you will likely have realized one thing: the Chinese love their tea. It's no news but an accepted fact.

Tea is not just a drink, it is a way of life that has been for centuries. All of China's large cities have tea markets, and Beijing, being the capital, has a tea market not only grand in terms of size but also in quality and style. The tea market is located on a street named Maliandao Tea Street. The street, located on the southwest side of the Xuanwu District in Beijing, is the perfect place to learn about China's tea culture. The street, which is 1,500 meters long, is where you will find the finest teas from throughout China; Anxi Tieguanyin Tea, West Lake Dragon Well Tea, Dongting Biluochun Tea, Huangshan Maofeng Tea, Pingshui Pinhead Tea, Qihong Tea, Dianhong Tea, Dahongpao Tea, and Taiwan's Dongding Oolong Tea. If you are a tea lover, you really need to visit this tea market.

There are different tea houses and shops that specialize in tea, and shops that specialize in tea related items such as calligraphy and paintings. Competition is high, and this makes prices very good; each business owner makes their individual location unique and appealing to potential customers. Many of these shop owners also own tea plantations, which helps to keep the prices low. The Maliandao Tea Street is also the perfect place for visitors with an extensive knowledge of tea, or those who are interested in but do not have a large knowledge of Chinese tea.

Tea shops always offer free tea to visitors and are always more than happy to offer suggestions, and tell tourists about the rich world of Chinese tea. It is more than just a drink, it is a huge component of Chinese culture. China has several styles of tea ceremonies and many different ways of brewing different teas. Visitors are advised to look around to compare prices before making any purchases.

This tea street is the largest tea distribution area in northern China. Retailers purchase tea here and export it to the United States, Korea, Russia, Japan, and many countries in the Middle East and Southeast Asia. It is truly a wonderful way to experience the Chinese culture.

DOS AND DONT'S IN CHINA

THINGS YOU DO NOT DO IN CHINA

A trip to China is definitely exciting and an eye-opener. Culture, manners, and social ideas might be quite different from your home country and you might need some time to get adjusted. The list below is filled with important points to take note of so as to avoid negative experiences with the local Chinese people and also to make your trip stress and trouble free.

1) DON'T DISRESPECT HOMES OR TEMPLES

It is very important to remove your shoes before entering many temples. However, when it comes to homes, this is a personal thing as Chinese follow different household customs. Therefore, you can ask your host if you should remove your shoes or not.

It is also rude to show the bottom of your feet or your soles to others in the Chinese culture. So when you sit and cross your legs, try to point your feet at a spot where there are no Chinese present.

2) DON'T BRING UP UNCOMFORTABLE TOPICS

Without having a substantial reason, don't talk about death, or mention someone who has died. Death is quite a serious topic to the Chinese. While white represents life and purity in most cultures, the color white represents death in China. Yes, quite ironic, so avoid giving white items as gifts or wrapping gifts in white paper or ribbons.

Other things you shouldn't talk about include such topics as comparing China to Japan, or political and religious issues. This is because Chinese people are often uncomfortable discussing history or political incidents that may cause embarrassment to China with foreigners, as they see their history from a different perspective. Avoiding sensitive topics like this will keep your conversation positive and friendly.

3) DON'T EXPECT WESTERN COMMUNICATION WITH THE LOCALS

When visiting a foreign country, you have to exercise patience. Don't expect the locals you encounter to speak English. It's also a good idea to pick up basic Chinese words and to try to communicate in the language of the region you are visiting.

Another thing you shouldn't do is to point at people or beckon with one finger when you are communicating with them. This is deemed rude and disrespectful. Instead, motion with the palm of your hand.

4) DON'T TOUCH PEOPLE

With the Chinese, touching, hugging, and kissing are done less compared with other cultures. These notions may go against your beliefs and what you are familiar with at home, where affection is much more readily displayed, but it is important to respect the culture of the country you are visiting. When you meet someone for the first time, it might be best to simply greet verbally. When greeting, a slight nod is fine. Don't kiss or hug hello or goodbye, as personal contact is quite unusual.

Due to tradition and religion in many areas of the country, the head is considered sacred. Be aware of this, and don't pat people on the head or play with their hair.

However, you'll find that personal space in public (especially on public transport) is quite uncommon. Chinese in crowds can be pushy and crush up against others for a place in line or a seat.

5) GIFTING

If you are traveling to China to meet individuals, either for business or personal reasons, you might consider gifting. Appropriate gifts given at appropriate times may be useful in building relationships.

It isn't usually considered appropriate in China to refuse a gift that is offered. However, don't be offended and don't stop offering if a gift is refused at first. Usually, it may require several offers before a gift is accepted. It is an aspect of Chinese culture to refuse the first offer – this is done to show restraint. Just make sure to give these gifts for the right reasons, so as not to come off as being offensive or offering a bribe.

6) DON'T OFFEND WITH YOUR GIFT

Gift baskets of flowers and fruits are common in the western world, but certain types of flowers and fruits are considered unlucky and inappropriate in China. If you are keen on giving these as gifts, you need to learn about the special meanings the Chinese people attribute to flowers and fruits to know what exactly to give.

•   Avoid dark and white colors since these are commonly associated with bad luck.

•   Do not give clocks as gifts since they remind the Chinese of death.

•   Green hats are prohibited as gifts. This is because the phrase "to wear a green hat" (戴绿帽子 dài lǜ màozi) means 'to be cuckold by one's unfaithful wife.'

•   Avoid giving anything in fours. This is because the Chinese word for four sounds like the word for death.

•   Do not give sharp objects as gifts because the Chinese people consider it to be bad luck.

On the contrary, eight sounds like the word 'fa', which means 'wealth' or 'good fortune.' Since eight is a lucky number, gifts that come in sets of eight are considered lucky.

Whenever somebody offers you their business card or a gift, make sure to accept it with both hands. The same applies if you are offering your business card or gift to someone else. This is seen as a sign of respect.

7) DO NOT GIVE TIPS

Tipping is one practice that is not usually observed in China. Cab drivers, restaurant staff, and other employees of labor do not expect to be tipped and could even be offended if offered a tip. If not offended, they will be confused and try to give your money back. Not tipping at all would, therefore, prevent these awkward situations. In some luxury hotels, tips are accepted, but they are not expected or demanded.

The only exception to this practice is during tours that are organized for tourists. The individuals on these tours often depend on tips for their income. So, it is okay to tip your tour guides.

8) DON'TS WHEN HOSTED BY A CHINESE

If you are a foreigner, the Chinese are not quite sure what you'll do when they invite you for a meal. It is considered rude if someone who isn't the host at the table starts ordering the food since the host gets to order all the dishes and usually does so without asking people what they want. But since you are a foreigner, it would probably be okay for you to tell the host what you like or dislike—this depends on the situation and who you are with.

It is important to know that in China, restaurant bills are never shared. It's their way of life; you don't go 'dutch' where bills are concerned. So if you have asked people out yourself, you are expected to pick up the entire bill.

9) DON'TS FOR TABLE MANNERS

Don't ignore chopsticks etiquette. The Chinese have many opinions on this issue. Chopsticks are meant for eating only, they are not to be used to gesture to items or persons. They are also not drumsticks, so do not use them for such purposes especially at the table.

When you are done with a meal, place the chopsticks on top of the bowl. It is imperative that you not stick your chopsticks straight up in the food because it is regarded as a bad sign that could represent death or a curse against them.

10) DON'T GET ANGRY

It is likely that something unexpected might happen during your trip, but it is advisable that you don't get angry and make a scene, as you could lose respect with the people involved; this will likely leave the situation unresolved. The best way to deal with situations like this in China is to remain calm and patient, and ask for help from your guide or a Chinese speaking individual that also understands English to solve the issue at hand.

THINGS TO DO WHEN IN CHINA

There are some places and some things that tourists shouldn't miss, such as climbing the Great Wall, cruising along the Yangtze River, cooking Chinese dishes, etc. Below we will discuss many of the major activities and places of interest in China.

1. A version of the Great Wall in Guiyang

There is a saying in China that "one who fails to reach the Great Wall is not a hero." Therefore, one of the must-see places to visit in China is the legendary Great Wall. Having a history of about 2000 years, it is the most supreme treasure of Chinese history and civilization. It is one of the most outstanding symbols of the country representing the people's heritage.

A Wall in Guiyang

2. EMBARK ON A YANGTZE RIVER CRUISE

The Yangtze River happens to be one of the world's most geographically, historically, and culturally important bodies of water. Also, the Yangtze is the longest river in Asia. Visitors can see the Yangtze by taking a cruise, which normally travels from Chongqing to Zhichang, or from Yichang to Chongqing. The prices for these inclusive journeys vary depending on the class of the cabin. Ticket prices usually include the cruise ticket as well as entrance fees to select sites of interest on both banks. For those looking for an even more luxurious Yangtze experience, there are some luxury cruises with only the most modern facilities and even more exquisite food. Cruises usually last for about 3 days.

3. PAY A VISIT TO THE TERRACOTTA ARMY IN XI'AN

The Terracotta Army in Xi'an was built to protect the tomb of China's first emperor, Emperor Qin Shi Huang. Going to China and not seeing the Terracotta Army is like going to New York and missing the Metropolitan Museum or like going to Egypt and not paying a visit to the Pyramid of Giza. Viewing Emperor Qin Shi Huang's immense Terracotta Army guarding his burial site and protecting his entry to the afterlife from the earthly side is certainly one of the most memorable parts of any trip to China. In 1987, the incredible mausoleum of the first emperor of China from the Qin Dynasty and his terracotta army was listed on the UNESCO World Heritage list.

Terra-cotta warriors in Xi'an

4. LEARN CHINESE KUNG FU IN SHAOLIN TEMPLE

Having seen a couple Chinese movies, you might want to learn about Kung Fu, and probably be like Jackie Chan or Jet Li. Now that you are in China, perhaps this is the time to give that dream a try. Chinese Kung Fu, also known as martial arts, is a traditional Chinese sport that developed from ancient times. Very rich in form and content, it includes a variety of different styles and methods. This art form is known to boost energy, fitness, coordination, mental well-being, self-discipline, and confidence because it requires coordination of the mind and body.

5. SEE THE GIANT PANDAS IN THE SICHUAN PROVINCE

Giant Pandas

~ 130 ~

Don't you just love those black and white pandas? Well, you're in luck as pandas are native to central-western and southwestern China. They are easily recognized by the large distinctive black patches around their eyes, ears, and on their rotund bodies. The Sichuan province has 30% of the pandas in the world. Pandas can eat up to 25 kg bamboos per day. The giant panda has long been a favorite of the public, at least partly on account that the species has an appealing baby-like cuteness that resembles that of a teddy bear. The fact that it is usually depicted reclining peacefully eating bamboo, as opposed to hunting, also adds to its image of innocence. Taking several pictures with this cute animal will be sure to make your day a blast!

6. LEARN TO COOK CHINESE FOOD

Your visit to China would be incomplete without you learning how to cook Chinese food. China happens to have an unbelievably large variety of cuisines with widely varying but fantastic and mouthwatering flavors; this is as a result of its diversity in climate, geography, and customs. Each of the local dishes has their unique characteristics. Chinese food is categorized into what is known as the 'Eight cuisine.' So take a simple course in making one Chinese meal, or take even more courses. This will also help you in eating healthy and not depending all the time on takeout food.

7. VISIT "798 ART DISTRICT" IN BEIJING

This is a vibrant culture space in the Chinese capital; a sort of Chinese Montmartre, full of art galleries, boutiques, exhibitions, nice cultural events. Art lovers adore this place, it is not even Asian, it is international. I would recommend you visit this area as well.

8. CELEBRATE THE CHINESE NEW YEAR (SPRING FESTIVAL)

How wonderful it would be for you to experience this festival during your trip to China. This holiday falls on the first day of the Chinese lunar calendar. The Chinese New Year celebration is China's biggest traditional holiday, and it runs for 15 days. The celebration is filled with lots of fun, festivities, and exquisite food. The Chinese New Year actually has a lot more to it than lion dances and firecrackers, although these aspects are integral to tradition. In many ways, this holiday is like Christmas to the West as it is about spending time with family, gift giving, and, above all, for celebrating the new season and its blessings.

9: DO SOME SHOPPING IN HONG KONG

Hong Kong's shopping is absolutely world renowned, and it's hard to beat. You get to shop wide and varied selections, low prices, and high quality, and as a foreigner, once you tender your passport, taxes are returned. Don't you just love it! Every year, billions of visitors from countries around the world go to Hong Kong to shop. Items are considered cheaper to buy in Hong

Kong when compared to the same items in the EU, USA, or Australia and therefore are very affordable.

THINGS CONSIDERED UNLUCKY IN CHINA

The Chinese believe a lot about good and bad luck. Now, as they say, "When in Rome, do as the Romans." Here are some tips on how to avoid bad luck in China.

1.   Do not turn over a fish if it's on a plate, as this is considered a bad omen. Preferably, use chopsticks to pull the flesh from beneath the fish.

2.   The number '4' is considered a number of bad luck, the reason being that Si (four) sounds like si (death). The use of this number is avoided as much as possible. It is hard to find a hospital with a ward four, and telephone numbers that include number four cost the least. High rise buildings quite often do not have floor 4, 14, etc.

3.   Cutting a pear in half for your lover is also considered a bad omen. This is because Fen li (to split a pear) also sounds like fen li (to depart). The belief is that the splitting of the pear may result in your relationship splitting up.

4.   While 7 is considered to be a lucky number in some cultures, this is quite the opposite in China. Seven is a yang number that is considered to be unlucky

because its pronunciation in Chinese is close to the pronunciation of the word meaning gone (去 qu). Seven can also be said to relate to ceremonies that release dead souls from purgatory.

WHAT TO BUY IN CHINA

Most countries are notable for specific purchase items. This also applies to China; there are just some things you should buy when you visit China. Remember, don't be in a hurry to buy everything, you will discover that each city has its own specialty. Some of the best buys in various cities are:

• Beijing: fresh water pearls, antiquities, semi-precious stones

• Shanghai: silk carpets

• Hangzhou: Longjing tea, silk

• Suzhou: silk

• Guilin: scroll paintings, South China Sea pearls

• Tibet: thangka (tanka: sheep skin wall hangings)

• Xi'an: replicas of the Terracotta Warriors, Tang Dynasty hand painted china, antique furniture

• Yunnan: mounted butterflies, Pu'er tea; Dali batik (tie-dyed fabric)

- Xinjiang: carpets, jade articles, dried fruit

- Guangzhou: wholesale markets for clothes, shoes, toys, electronic products and more.

TOP SOUVENIRS FOR A FIRST-TIME TRAVELER TO CHINA

- Art — papercuttings, paintings, photos, postcards, scrolls

- Rice writing — your name on a grain of rice

- Pretty umbrellas for the rain or sun.

- Mahjong tile set

- Panda souvenirs

- Silk

- Tea

GLASSES AND CONTACTS

Glasses and contacts are pretty cheap in China, so it's worth stocking up, especially if you like to have a bunch of different stylish glasses designs. Glasses sold at opticians throughout the city tend to be of decent quality, but not exactly brand names. In Beijing, there is a special glasses market near Panjiayuan's antiques market. The biggest one in Shanghai is located near the railway station.

Beijing Glasses City, 43 Huawei Beili, Panjiayuan, Dongsanhuan Nanlu, Chaoyang District, Beijing.Shanghai Ye Optical Glasses Market, Shanghai Train Plaza South Square, 4-5F, 360 Meiyuan Lu, Zhabei District, Shanghai.

ACCESSORIES AND JEWELRY

China is perfect for purchasing accessories and jewelry. Most markets and tourist attractions have shops that sell everything from bracelets and necklaces to rings and jade accessories. It is important to note that most items picked up in tourist markets or at tourist sites might not be real silver or jade, hence the quality will not be incredibly high. However, if you bargain well enough, it'll be worth it.

TAILORING AND CLOTHES

Tailored clothes are really cheap in China, so lots of people choose to have their clothes made while in China because it is so much cheaper than having a dress made back at home. However, make sure you know what fabric and style you want.

LEATHER GOODS

You will find all kinds of leather goods in China. Many of the markets sell leather bags and belts at prices much cheaper than most western countries. To show that their products are of good quality, many vendors use a lighter to demonstrate how their bags, wallets, and belts do not melt when exposed to flame. Make sure to get the specific item that has been tested, and not a new one pre-packaged that may be of a different quality. In Beijing and

Shanghai, big markets have plenty of products to choose from. In Guangzhou, visit the Sanyuanli Leather market.

* Beijing Silk Street Market

* Shanghai's Shopping

* Guangzhou 78 Sanyuanli Dadao, Baiyun District, Guangzhou

TOILETS IN CHINA

You think everything in China is different from what you are used to? Wait until you see the toilets. The squat toilet is the regularly used toilet. There are advantages and disadvantages to this type of toilet. The squat toilet is considered to be more sanitary than western toilets because you don't have to touch anything—well, unless you fall in. The con for foreigners is the fact that your leg muscles are not used to squatting. It doesn't mean there are no western toilets in China; however, they may not be as sanitary as their counterparts.

CHINA TRAVEL TIPS ON TOILETS

•   Squat toilets are widely used all over China, but sometimes you just need to look for a sign that signifies a western type of toilet.

•   Keep toilet paper or tissues with you at all times; most public toilets do not provide toilet paper. The toilet paper you might find in public restrooms is usually the typical Chinese style, which is thick, pink, and sandpaper-like. Some toilets have toilet paper dispensers near the sinks at the entrance, not in the stalls. Many toilets have an automatic water flush system.

•   Try to practice squatting at home before your trip.

• Need a western sit down toilet? Go to a hotel (Chinese or Western Chains) or museum (check the handicap stall). KFC, Pizza Hut, McDonald's, and Starbucks will most likely have the squat one.

• Major airports have western toilets, but smaller airports may have squat toilets.

• Do not put used paper in the toilets; make sure to use the waste basket next to the toilet.

• Use terms like "toilets" or "wash closets" (WC), as opposed to "bathroom" or "restroom," the people are more conversant with those terms.

• Knock the toilet door before opening. This is because many people do not lock the door from inside or there is no lock at all.

Toilet Instructions

CREDIT CARDS AND CASH IN CHINA

China is very much about the use of cash. Credit cards are mostly used at hotels, big restaurants, and malls, but expect to pay cash when you visit places like the market, small restaurants, and when taking taxis, unless you like paying a great deal more than you need to because you will be charged an additional fee for card use.

You'll find cards are of minimal use when doing most shopping, and even where conventional stores attempt to take them, they require you show your passport. You may also encounter problems unless your card is chip-and-pin, although this isn't a problem when using the automated teller machine.

You don't have to change your currency to CN¥ before leaving home, as most times the rate will be awful and outrageous. There are plenty of change options at the major international airports, there are multiple ATMs that change hard currency into local currency, and bank exchange counters are open long hours.

The best bet is to travel with a bank card (ATM card), having first checked what system your card uses and consulted your card issuer as to the locations of compatible ATMs. Machines accepting foreign cards with instructions in English are much more numerous than they used to be. In the major cities, as long as your bank card is on systems like Cirrus or Plus, you'll have no difficulties.

You should ask your bank what it is charging as the exchange rate, but most of the time it is lower than the tourist rate. Also, there shouldn't be any problem in withdrawing whatever amount of cash is needed since Chinese bank machines let you make multiple withdrawals on the same day. Machines in China typically limit you to ¥2000-¥2500 per withdrawal ($290–$370), although in the metropolises you can find machines of Citibank, HSBC, Deutsche Bank, etc., which offer you the same limit as you have at home.

Fraud is a huge problem in China, so it is important to alert your bank and credit card company that you're going to be in China to avoid being declined.

MUST SEE IN BEIJING

Beijing formerly known as 'Peking' is the capital of China. It is city that has been the heart of China's history for centuries. Located in the northern part of China, Beijing is a place of revolution, and it is transforming itself for the 21st century at full tilt. There is so much to see and do here. There are just some places you must see when you go to Beijing.

The Great Wall of China

This is one of the seven wonders of the world. Built originally to keep the invading Mongol forces out, the Great Wall has come to represent China itself. It is one of the biggest tourist attractions in the world and can be gotten to via a day trip from Beijing. You can learn a lot about this amazing structure by taking one of the tours organized by professional tour operators or a hotel.

The Forbidden City

Forbidden City

A visit to the Forbidden City is a must! This was the palace of the Emperors for more than 500 years from the Ming Dynasty to the Qing dynasty. It currently houses the Palace Museum. In this museum are countless appealing antiques. What is more amazing is that the city can be easily accessed as it is in the center of Beijing.

Other notable places to visit in Beijing are the Lama Temple, Temple of Heaven, Summer Palace, Don, Drum and Bell Towers, etc. One other thing to try out is the local dish of Peking Duck; many restaurants serve this dish, just visit any of the local Chinese restaurants and you will be treated with this fantastic food and at a great price.

MUST SEE SHOWS IN BEIJING

1.   THE LEGEND OF KUNG FU

• Venue: Red Theater 红剧场

• Address: Workers' Cultural Palace, 44 Xingfu Dajie, Chongwen District

• Booking: 010-67103671/72/73

• Show time: 19:30-20:30 daily

• Ticket price: RMB 180-680

This show revolves around the story of a young boy found wandering outside an ancient temple in China, who dreams of becoming a Kung Fu master. It is a wonderful mix of dance and Kung Fu arts, and is bound to be a stunning and exciting experience for you as part of your China tour.

2.   PEKING OPERA

• Venue: Liyuan Theater 梨园剧场

• Address: 1/F Qianmen Hotel, 175 Yongan Road, Hufangqiao

• Show time: 19:30-20:50 daily

• Phone: 86-10-63016688

• Ticket price: RMB 180-680

Extremely popular in the Qing Dynasty court, Peking opera is now regarded as one of the cultural treasures of China. In Peking opera, you can find English subtitles, Chinese acrobatics, and some colorful dance performances.

3. NEW PEKING OPERA: THE FORBIDDEN LOVE

• Venue: Minorities Cultural Palace Theater 民族文化宫

• Address: 49 Fuxingmen Neidajie, Xidan/Financial Street 复兴门内大街 49 号

• Show time: 7:30 pm - 9:15 pm daily

• Booking line: 86-10-66088077

• Price: RMB 180, 280, 380, 480, 580

Some unique things about this opera house are its innovative stage design, its top of the line lighting and video equipment as well as the modern choreography merged with acrobatics and martial arts. The plot is an adaptation of the Song dynasty folktale "Madame White Snake."

4. ACROBATICS SHOW at TIANDI THEATER

• Venue: Tiandi Theater 天地剧场

- Address: No.10 Dongzhimen Nanjie

- Show time: 17:30-18:40 and 19:30 -20:40 daily

- Price: RMB 180, 280, 380, 480

This show covers a large variety of fields: acrobatics, aerial acts, farce, vocal imitations, magic, etc. With this show, you get the very best as the troupe is one of the best and largest acrobatic circuses with one of the most comprehensive programs in China.

5. PEKING OPERA at HUGUANG GUILD HALL

- Venue: Huguang Guild Hall 湖广会馆

- Address: Hufang Lu 3, xuanwu District. Subway Line 2 Heping Men (exit D1); walk south 10 min

- Show time: 19:30-20:45 daily

- Tel: 86-10-63518284

- Ticket price: RMB 180-380

This opera house was built in 1807. At the height of its glory, the Huguang Guild Hall was known as one of the "Four Great Theatres" of Beijing. Many famous past and present opera performers have performed here. Peking opera and many other local performances are shown here every day. In addition, a small museum is contained in the Huguang Guild Hall, which exhibits the theater's rich history of Beijing opera.

6. KUN QU OPERA: THE PEONY PAVILION

• Venue: The Imperial Granary 皇家粮仓

• Address: Nanxincang, 22 Dongsishitiao, Chaoyang District

• Show time: Every Friday and Saturday at 19:30

• Ticket price: RMB 380, 580, 780, 980, 1980, and RMB 12000 for a 6-8 people compartment. A Cantonese-style buffet will be provided free to the audience one hour ahead of the performance.

• Tel: 86-10-64096499

Listed as an item of UNESCO intangible world heritage, Kun Qu is one of the oldest forms of Chinese opera still performed today. This play, one of China's best-loved classical operas, is a love story that was written during the Ming Dynasty and was first performed in 1598. Today it is a regular performance, but only about 60 visitors are admitted into the small but ancient Imperial Granary. Hopefully, you're lucky enough to be one of those sixty or thereabout.

7. MONGOLIAN DANCE AND MUSIC SHOWS

• Venue: Tenggeli Tala 腾格里塔拉

• Address: Xicui Lu, 1000m north of Shagou Lukou 西翠路, 沙沟路口北 1000 米路东

- Tel: 86-10-68150808 68150706

- Show time: 19:30-20:30

- Price: RMB 316 for night show and RMB 518 for VIP seats; RMB 188 for lunch show at 12:15-13:00.

This includes a spectacular Mongolian dance, music performances, dishes such as whole roasted sheep, as well as a generous buffet piled high with endless variations of mutton and salads. The theater restaurant's performing troupe always leaves the audience stunned with their show of Ordos Wedding. This show displays the lives of the Mongolians, with talented singers, dancers, and performers.

TRAVEL AGENCIES IN CHINA

China is so vast, and there are just too many places to see and things to do. To get the best out of your trip to China, I advise that you employ the services of a good travel agency.

Travel agencies across China are moving beyond the traditional elements of a holiday, like visiting Beijing, Great Wall, Yangtze cruise, and the Terracotta Army. Since there is now a demand among international travelers for the traditional China experience, the inclination is now towards more variety. Hence, regions such as Yunnan in the southwest, with its stone forest, are now regularly found in travel agency websites. Unfamiliar regions such as the white sand dunes of Gansu province or the Birthplace of Confucius in Shandong province are also being promoted.

An increasing number of travel agencies offer customized packages based on travelers' individual interests as well as budget. Travel agencies like the China Tour Service www.chinatoursservice.netoffers and China Custom Tours www.chinacustomstours.com with associates in China and the United States offer special-interest tours. The China Culture Center www.chinaculturecenter.com provides trips off the beaten path.

So wherever you want to go, be it to get a feel of what ancient China was, or to take in the fast-paced growth of modern China, it is convenient and advised to retain the services of a good travel agency.

Sand Dunes in Gansu Province

CHINESE MASSAGE

Chinese massage is in a way similar to acupuncture. It is believed by ancient Chinese experts and practitioners that when energy in the body flows steadily, it helps the process of stress relief and can even prevent some diseases. There exists two major types of traditional Chinese massage: the "Tui na" and the "Zhi Ya." Though the techniques between these two differ, the general feeling of renewed strength and vigor is experienced after a session of at least 30 minutes. Chinese massage techniques have become widely used around the world.

CHINESE MASSAGE TECHNIQUES

The "Tui na" technique requires stretching, kneading, and pushing the muscles, while the "Zhi Ya" involves pressing and pinching acupressure points to relieve stress and pain. Each technique is based on therapeutic principles with effects such as stimulation of the body into producing more hormones, regulation of blood flow, and boosting energy or recovery. Hand techniques are further categorized into the sedating techniques known as "yin" and the stimulating techniques known as "yang." The idea is to balance both yin and yang to achieve full health.

BENEFITS OF CHINESE MASSAGE

Chinese massage therapy provides pain relief from injured muscles. As a result of Chinese massage, blood flow improves to areas, which in turn facilitates health. It also helps to produce a calm and relaxing mood. Regular massage sessions boost immunity and prevent the body from developing degenerative diseases.

BEST MASSAGE PLACES IN BEIJING

A.   BEST FOR IRONING OUT ACHES AND PAINS

i.   Tang Massage

Go for Chinese massage (168RMB; 45 minutes.

8-2 Jiaodaokou Dong Dajie (8402 4408). Open 10am-2am daily.

ii.   Suhang Blind Massage

Massages from 80RMB.

Go for Full Body Massage (80RMB; one hour). The skilled therapist meticulously examines your body, targeting all your sore spots while finding a few new ones you didn't catch.

 9 Gongti Dong Lu (5607 8788). Open 9am-11:30pm daily.

iii.   Song Lin

Massages from 80RMB.

Go for Body and Foot Massage (138RMB; two hours).

Third Floor, 15 Zaoying Beili, off Maizidian Jie (6585 1338). Open 10am-3am daily.

B.   BEST FOR REDUCING STRESS

i.   Zigzag Massage

Massages from 138RMB.

Go for Foot Reflexology Massage (138RMB; one hour).

52B Wudaoying Hutong (8404 0020). Open 11am-11pm daily.

C.   BEST FOR LUXURY ON A BUDGET

i.   Bodhi Therapeutic Retreat

A cross between a deluxe version of your local massage place and an indulgent spa. At Bodhi, it's all about the downtime. With its Southeast Asia-inspired décor, it's a little bit of luxury in the middle of Sanlitun. Essential oils, bathtubs, fluffy towels, and plush sheets, along with a team of attentive Chinese and Thai massage therapists, make for an experience that's all sorts of serene. You can even order some food from the neighborhood.

Massages from 198RMB. If you are with a group, bring 10 coupons.

Go for Foot Reflexology Treatment (80mins; 188RMB). While you stuff your face with free snacks, massage therapists start with a relaxing back-and-head massage before tending to your weary feet.

7 Gongti Bei Lu (6417 9595). Open 11am-00:30am daily.

ii.   Dragonfly Therapeutic Retreat

Once you cross the threshold into the sanctuary that is Dragonfly, it's difficult not to spend the entire day there. A far cry from your basic massage spot, this Beijing favorite and well-known chain is an oasis of calm, where silence is only broken by the classic spa sounds playing through the speakers. It's all soft lighting, cushy beds, and incense. Here you get what you pay for as professional staff set to work to ease all your aches and pains.

Massages from 188RMB.

Go for Oriental Foot Massage (188RMB; one hour).

Grand Summit Plaza (100m north of Lufthansa Centre), 19 Dongfang Dong Lu (8532 3132). Open 10am-midnight daily.

INVITATIONS TO DRINK TEA

Serving tea is a custom in China and has a long history of about 3000 years. Since the Zhou Dynasty, tea has been a kind of present between friends and relatives and tribute for royalty. It is a tradition. According to Chinese traditional culture, no matter where the venue is, serving tea must relate to tea etiquette. The steps of serving tea:

- Smell the tea. The host should show the tea, and introduce the characteristics to guests, while guests should smell the tea in turns.

- Warm the teapot. Fill the boiled water into the empty pot to warm the pot, then pour out the water.

- Fill the tea into the pot. According to the variety of the tea, scoop the quantity of the tea. Use teaspoon to scoop the tea, not the hand.

- Invite guest to drink. Use two hands to hold the tea to guests to show respect. The tea cup should be put into the right hand of the guest. Fill the water again when the water is nearly drank out. As a guest, you should appreciate the tea and try to avoid drinking a big mouthful of tea.

- Try to avoid crossing legs when drinking tea no matter whether you're the host or guest.

TEA SERVING ETIQUETTE IN CHINA

Antique Chinese Tea Pot

Serving guests with tea is a daily etiquette in social life and family life in ancient China. There are some tips for serving tea to your guest or an elder:

- When it is served, the tea shoudn't be filled to the brim of the cup.

- The water should not be too hot.

- If there are more than 2 guests, the color of tea should be almost the same for both guests.

- When serving refreshments, put them directly in front of the guest while the tea cup should be placed to the right of the refreshments.

- When serving tea, hold the cup with your right hand and offer from the right side of the guest with a smile.

- The same tea leaves can serve up to 3 or 4 cups. When a guest's cup is empty, the host is expected to refill the cup.

Tea plantations

SOCIALIZING IN CHINA

When westerners prepare to move out to China, one of their biggest worries is that they will struggle to make friends. However, do not be worried as Chinese people are quite friendly and entertaining.

There are lots of unique Chinese ways to 玩儿 (wán (r)) –

hang out, or play. Below are examples of ways of socializing in China that are really fun and are great ways to build close friendships with Chinese people.

1. 麻将 *(MÁ JIANG) – MAHJONG*

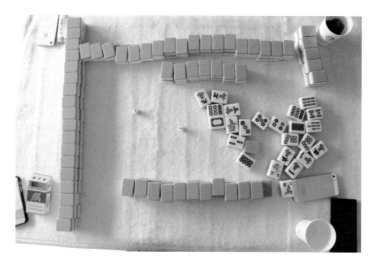

Mahjong

Life in China is full of games. Whether you're active and into ping pong or prefer to use your strategic skills in a game of cards, you'll always find a Chinese person keen to play with you.

Ask most people to name a Chinese game and they'll say "麻将 (má jiang) – mahjong. It's true that 麻将 (má jiang) is played pretty much everywhere in China, from luxurious specially designed parlors in five star hotels to old outdoor tables in the local park. 麻将 (má jiang) is played with 144 tiles and four players.

Initially, it looks terrifyingly complicated! When in fact, players take turns picking up and discarding tiles to try to create a winning hand. Like most good games, it combines strategy and skill with an element of luck.

Although gambling is technically illegal in China, Chinese often play for small amounts of money. If you're invited to join in, it's definitely a good idea to spend a couple of hours watching first to get the hang of the game, or get some practice on one of the many online mahjong sites.

2. DO IT LIKE A 东北人 (DŌNG BĚI RÉN) – NORTHEASTERNER: STREETSIDE BARBECUE AND BEER

After dark in a Chinese city, customers sit at small tables next to the barbecue with kebabs and vegetables, washing their food down with cups of local 啤酒 (pí jiǔ) – beer, or 白酒 (bái jiǔ) – usually translated as "white wine," but it's actually hard liquor.

This style of eating and drinking is usually associated with China's 东北人 (dōng běi rén) – Northeasterners, who have a well-deserved reputation for being the best drinkers; streetside barbecue and beer has now spread all over the country!

Chinese drinking culture is quite different from that in Western countries - people share bottles and toast each other by shouting 干杯 (gān bēi) cheers and downing their drinks together. 干杯 (gān bēi) literally means "dry the cup," but fortunately Chinese people tend to drink out of much smaller cups.

3. ULTIMATE SOCIAL FOOD: 火锅 (HUǑ GUŌ) – HOTPOT

Hotpot 火锅 (huǒ guō) involves boiling fresh ingredients in a huge shallow pot of broth, usually flavored with chilis, garlic, or both. It's a super sociable way of eating as everyone helps to cook by adding ingredients to the pot, and the food is fresh and tasty.

Tip: If handling uncooked meat, clean your chopsticks by leaving them in the boiling broth for a minute.

Seafood in China is usually so fresh that it's alive until you cook it, so keep this in mind when going for seafood hotpot.

Even though eating out in China is super affordable and delicious, many Chinese still like to entertain friends at home. When invited to a Chinese home to eat, it's a good idea to bring some fruit or snacks for your hosts, and expect to be asked to change into a pair of slippers when you arrive.

4.   KTV: IT'S NOT KARAOKE LIKE WE KNOW IT

In fact, 唱歌 (chàng gē) – singing in a karaoke club is one

of the most common ways for young Chinese people to hang out.

Thankfully, "KTV" (Chinese-style karaoke) is not like western karaoke. Instead of testing your musical skills in front of a large room full of strangers, KTV involves booking a small, private room for just you and your friends. You use a machine to select songs and order drinks and snacks from the many waiters and waitresses standing outside.

TV CHANNELS IN CHINA

Watching TV is a favorite way of passing the time. When bored or stressed out, sitting in front of the TV and watching your favorite programs can be a very pleasant feeling. Here is a list of the top 10 most popular TV channels in China. These channels have the highest ratings; however, just like most communication in China, most of the broadcasts are done in Chinese.

1. CCTV 中央电视台

CCTV is China's state television broadcaster. It made its debut in 1958. With 22 channels broadcasting to China and the world, broadcasts are done in languages such as Chinese, English, Spanish, and Russian.

Website: http://english.cntv.cn/01/index.shtml

2. HUNAN SATELLITE TELEVISION 湖南卫视

This is China's most popular provincial TV station. It is also China's second most-watched channel, second only to CCTV. The channel features various TV shows as well as exclusive TV series.

Website: http://www.hunantv.com/

PRACTICAL TIPS TO LIVE OR TRAVEL IN CHINA

3. PHOENIX SATELLITE TELEVISION 凤凰卫视

This television channel is a Hong Kong-based Chinese television broadcaster. It serves mainland China, Hong Kong, and other areas where Chinese live around the world.

Website: http://www.ifeng.com/

4. SHANGHAI ORIENTAL TELEVISION 东方卫视

Shanghai Oriental Television features news, sports, education, arts, movies, and plays.

Website: https://zh.wikipedia.org/zh/%E4%B8%9C%E6%96%B9% E5%8D%AB%E8%A7%86

5. JIANGSU SATELLITE TELEVISION 江苏卫视

Based in Nanjing city, this is a provincial channel.

Website: http://www.jstv.com/

6. ZHEJIANG TELEVISION 浙江卫视

Zhejiang Television is Zhejiang province's provincial TV channel. "The Voice of China," a popular singing contest program made this channel famous.

Website:http://www.zjstv.com/

7. SHENZHEN SATELLITE TV 深圳卫视

This TV is based in Shenzhen, Guangdong province. The channel broadcasts Chinese music, news, and Chinese talk shows.

Website: http://sztv.cutv.com/special/sztv.html

8. THE TRAVEL CHANNEL 旅游卫视

Covering travel, news, fashion, entertainment, and many other fields, the Travel Channel is China's national tourism satellite TV channel. The Travel Channel is located in Haikou, Hainan Province.

Website:http://www.tctc.com.cn/

9. ANHUI TV 安徽卫视

Beginning its broadcast in 1960, Anhui Television is a television network in Hefei, Anhui province. It currently broadcasts in Mandarin.

Website:http://www.ahtv.cn/

10. XING KONG TV 星空卫视

Xing Kong TV is a Mandarin language TV channel that covers drama series, comedies, variety talk shows, and game shows. Xing Kong is currently available in Mainland

China, Hong Kong, Macau, and some other countries in Southeast Asia.

Website:http://www.xingkong.com.cn/

You could also watch CNN, BBC, TV5, DISCOVERY, and other western channels in China with special prepaid packages.

FINDING AN AYI - OR A BABYSITTER IN CHINA

You might think of your ayi (阿姨, literally 'auntie') as a housekeeper, cleaner or nanny. Whatever you hire them for, they can be an incredible support, helping take the pressure off you domestically. Here's what you should know before you go looking for one.

THINGS TO CONSIDER

- What level of care do you require? Cleaning? Cooking? Doing laundry? Babysitting or taking care of pets?

- What specific tasks do you need your ayi to carry out? Do you know how to describe these in Chinese (You should prepare to, if you expect your ayi to do a good job)?

- How often do you need an ayi to visit, and for how long?

- How much are you willing to pay?

WAYS OF FINDING AN AYI OR BABYSITTER

- Getting a recommendation from a friend or colleague.

- Local expat websites may have classifieds sections or forums where you can browse or ask for help.

- Post fliers in the apartment complex where you live to look for candidates. Some grocery stores popular among expats may have notice boards where you can post an ad.

- Use a housekeeping agency. This will cost money, but you may find better-trained or even English-speaking ayi through these.

INTERVIEWING YOUR POTENTIAL AYI OR BABYSITTER

Next, arrange an interview with potential candidates. Make sure a Chinese speaker is there to help you, and think carefully about what you want to ask, and what you want to look out for. A few considerations to help guide you:

- Is she (ayi are pretty much always female) experienced in the tasks you're hiring her for?

- Do you trust her to keep your house clean and safe? Can she be relied on to look after your baby, children or pets?

- How old is she? You might have more faith in an older ayi.

- Is she neat and tidy?

- Does she have any qualifications or recommendations that prove her skills? This is unlikely, but it is worth considering.

- Can she speak English? To what level?

- Why does she want to work for expats?

- What can she cook?

- What did she do for previous employer(s)?

- How many people were there in her previous employer(s) house?

- Does she have children? Are they in the same city as you live in? Try to assess how much childcare experience the ayi has. Some ayi may be migrant workers who have children back in their hometown who are being taken care of by the ayi's family. Therefore, her own experience may be limited.

YOUR OBLIGATIONS

- Make clear what tasks she is expected to carry out. Be specific on both the tasks, how regular these tasks are (every time she visits? Daily? Weekly? At what time should these tasks be performed), and the standard you expect.

- Be clear about her working conditions – which day(s) do you need her to come? At a specific time? How long do you expect her to stay? When will she be paid, how and how much? Will you provide cleaning materials, or do you expect her to bring them? Will she have a key (and door card, if you need one to access your complex or building)?

WeChat app helps a lot to communicate with your ayi as it provides a translation of your messages.

SMOKING IN CHINA

Smoking in China is very prevalent, as China is not only the largest consumer but also the largest producer of tobacco. With 350 million Chinese smokers, China produces 42% of the world's cigarettes. The China National Tobacco Corporation (中国烟草总公司 Zhōngguó Yāncǎo Zǒnggōngsī) is by sales the largest single manufacturer of tobacco products in the world and boasts a monopoly in Mainland China generating between 7 and 10% of government revenue. Furthermore, outside the largest cities in China, smoking is considered socially acceptable anywhere at any time, though it is technically illegal.

The Chinese Association on Tobacco Control (中国控制吸烟协会 Zhōngguó kòngzhì xīyān xiéhuì) is engaged in tobacco control by members of the voluntary sector, including academic, social and mass organizations, as strong enforcement of existing tobacco control laws is not supported by the Chinese Government.

Smoking is a social custom in the China. Also, giving cigarettes at any social interaction is a sign of respect and friendliness. So, feel free to take a smoke (if you are a smoker) whenever you are in China.

SCAM ALERTS TO LOOK OUT FOR IN CHINA

Here are some of the most common scams that you might come across in China. One can never be too careful when it comes to issues like this, so make sure to take note.

THE ART SCHOOL SCAM

This is usually played out by a seemingly enthusiastic art student who approaches you in the street. These youngsters speak good English, so they are actually quite convincing. After engaging you, he/she then invites you to visit their studio to view original art pieces.

Most times they give you every reason to buy their masterpieces, keep in mind the prices are normally outrageous. Even if you are not necessarily interested, you might feel obliged to buy since they sometimes employ the use of emotional empathy. Plus, these young artists are usually good looking so you may think they are well off and therefore cannot possibly be scammers.

A simple "no thank you" is all that is required to prevent this somewhat common practice in Xi'an, Shanghai, and Beijing, More often than not, you will see the same piece of art the "art student" tried to sell you being sold at ridiculously low prices at a souvenir shop or in the street markets.

THE FAKE TAXI RIDE

When taking a taxi in China, sometimes the vehicle does look like a taxi but is in the actual sense a private car. Unofficial taxi drivers are common in pretty much all countries, and China happens to not be an exception. As soon as you enter a cab, make sure to check that the meter is actually running and if it's not, just get out as soon as it is safe. If you chose to remain inside, register the vehicle's details, such as the registration number and vehicle type, and if you end up paying much more than the regular fee, you can report the incident to the police. Taxis in the major cities of China are clearly marked. In smaller cities though, even marked taxis may want to negotiate on fare and not use the meter, just make sure to get the best price, whatever the situation is.

Another scam to beware of with taxi drivers is the fake money game. When you hand over your fare, the driver takes it and announces that "It is a fake one!" then actually returns to you a fake currency instead of the one you gave originally. Do not take it, threaten to call the police. This usually helps, also keep smaller notes ready since most of these fake notes are ¥ 50 and ¥100.

TEA HOUSE SCAM

A young Chinese student or two will approach you offering to show you around personally, as a way of improving their English, which they just happen to be studying. They may sometimes indicate that they are visiting as well, either from Taiwan or Hong Kong, and are tourists.

They then proceed to invite you for tea at a convenient restaurant close by, and by the time the bill has to be settled, your "host" is nowhere to be found. There's little or no point in arguing with the non-English speaking restaurant staff, even the police are of little or no help in such situations. You end up paying an outrageous amount. In Beijing, these types of scammers are common in and around Tiananmen Square and the Forbidden City, so keep this in mind when you go touring.

SHOPPING SCAMS

When shopping, look out for friendly strangers who approach you offering or insisting on rendering help to you in numerous ways. It could be to help you with your shopping and then transportation. In exchange, they will offer to teach you basic Chinese while you help them expand their English vocabulary. Most times these are accomplished scam artists, and often good-looking young ladies, so make sure to keep all conversations clear of private information.

Here are some other ways you can use to avoid a scam:

- Before purchase of any goods, payment for accommodation or acceptance of services, agree on a price. Make sure to keep your proof of payment handy at all times.

- Politely make sure to avoid answering questions posed by strangers such as "Which hotel are you staying at?" "What are your plans for your stay here?"

- Never show your cash in public; keep it out of sight. It would be best to put the amount of money you feel is needed for the day in a separate place that is close within your reach.

- Treat any stranger who's keen on showing you something special but strictly with you only with suspicion. They could be trying to move you to a remote place in preparation for a scam.

- Keep your identity confidential. For example, luggage labels, travel documents, tickets or anything that can reveal your name to strangers should be concealed.

- Be firm and avoid persistent strangers who may chose to ignore your request that they go away or leave you alone.

LEAVING CHINA

Documents to Prepare When Leaving China:

By now you must have had an amazing and memorable time during your stay in China. But everything comes to an end, and now it is the time to head back home. To leave China, foreigners need to have their valid passports, visa, credentials, and other documents checked by the border inspection office. If there's any hand baggage, this has to be examined by the Chinese Customs. In addition, foreigners are required to fill out a Departure Card and a Customs Declaration Form before leaving. It is important to leave China within the duration of time stated on the visa.

Can I Take the Things Bought From China Out?

Most definitely, as long as these items don't fall under the category of prohibited items and the amount you take is reasonable.

How Much Money Can I Take When Leaving?

As long as the amount of money you are taking out does not exceed the amount you brought into China, customs will let you go. Although if there isn't any record, you should not take more than USD10,000 or equivalent in any other currencies. You also need to declare

USD5,000-10,000 or equivalent in any other currencies with a Foreign Currency Holding Permit issued by the bank. Customs clearance is for cash less than and including USD5,000 or equivalent in any other currencies.

Prohibited Items to Leave With

•	Various weapons, simulated weapons, ammunition, and explosive devices

•	Forged currency and forged securities

•	Press items, roll film, photographs, phonograph disc, video disc, tape, video tape, laser video disc, laser audio disc, computer storage medium, and other items that can be harmful to the country's politics, economy, culture, and social morals

•	Deadly poisons

•	Addictive substances, including, opium, morphine, heroin, hemp, as well as other narcotics and psychotropic drugs

•	Priceless relics and other museum pieces whose export is prohibited

•	Endangered plants and their specimens, seeds, as well as materials for reproduction

•	Manuscript, roll film, photographs, phonograph disc, video disc, tape, video tape, laser video disc, laser audio disc, computer storage medium and other items related to the official secrets of the country

Who Will be Prohibited From Exiting?

•   Defendants in criminal cases and suspects who are accused by the Chinese public security organizations, the People's Procurator or the People's Court.

•   People having pending court cases.

•   Those who have violated Chinese laws and are still in the process of prosecution.

•   Those who hold invalid exit credentials, including forged, altered or another's credentials.

•   Those who refuse the border inspection of China.

•   Those who do not exit through the appointed exit port.

•   Those considered to be carrying contraband goods.

Conclusion

The purpose of this book was to prepare you well for a visit or your relocation to China. By now you are really well informed and know what to expect. China is a continent itself, full of surprises and challenges. I am always surprised by how few foreigners I meet while traveling through this amazing country. It has and offers so much, we just need to discover and enjoy it. I believe having read this book, you are more prepared to visit it.

INTERESTED IN GETTING MY BOOKS FOR FREE?

Then you are invited to join my First Readers & Reviewers group, which is entitled to get current and future books free. As a member, you will be able to choose to get a free e-copy of a book of your choice to read and review for Amazon.com or other websites.

How to apply?

It is easy – please send a message to ama37676@gmail.com with the following information:

Which of my books have you read already?

Link to your Amazon review of this book.

Can you commit to reading my new book in 5-7 days and giving me feedback?

I really value the opinion of my readers, so I always want to hear from you and to improve to better meet your expectations. I am always glad to hear from you! Let me know what you think.

Printed in Poland
by Amazon Fulfillment
Poland Sp. z o.o., Wrocław

65240206R00114